MW01611119

# Order
# My Steps

40-week devotional journal
for those who are longing to
be closer to God and to have
Him lead their daily lives

**Psalm 119:133**
**"Order my steps in thy word..."**

**LIANE R. GRANT**

Copyright © 2005 by Liane R. Grant
Revised Edition Copyright © 2017 by Liane R. Grant
Published by The King's Translators (Traducteurs du Roi),
a subsidiary of Mission Montréal.
544 Mauricien, Trois-Rivières (Québec) Canada   G9B 1S1
www.TraducteursduRoi.com

Layout: Jonathan Grant

All scripture quotations are from the King James Version of
the Holy Bible

**ISBN 978-2-924148-32-7**
Legal Deposit – Bibliothèque et Archives nationales du
Québec, 2017.
Legal Deposit – Library and Archives Canada, 2017.

# PREFACE

Are you longing for a deeper daily relationship with God?
Maybe you are a new Christian wondering what should
come next in your life. Or maybe you have been serving the
Lord for several years, but feel like you need to re-establish
your spiritual priorities. Just as an infant takes 40 weeks
to develop and grow in the womb, my prayer is that this
40-week devotional journal will be a spiritual rebirth for
you. Step by step, you will clarify God's desire for your life
and walk into all that He has planned for you.
Let Him order your steps!
(Psalm 119:133)

# ACKNOWLEDGEMENTS

To **Scott**: my husband and encourager. I learned most of these principles under your gentle ministry. I love you so much!

To **Mom, and Dad** (who's gone on ahead): Thanks for raising me right in a mixed-up world. Your quiet example has impacted me for eternity.

Most importantly, to **JESUS**: I wouldn't even consider life without you; there would be nothing left of me. I am amazed at Your love and grace; and how You have kept Your hand on my life and have been so patient as I learn to know You better.

# INTRODUCTION

Has God been tugging on your heart to draw closer to Him? Has He given you a glimpse of a special work He wants you to do for Him? Even with exciting promises in our hearts, it seems so hard to bridge the gap between desire and action: between longing for spiritual fulfillment and actually experiencing it.

This devotional journal is for people who are hungering to get closer to God, and to be useful in His kingdom. Perhaps you have watched and admired someone who seems to live that way, and you realize that God has more for your life than what you are experiencing right now.

How do you get to the place where God can use you? It would be awesome if it could happen overnight — as a stunning miracle! However, more often than not, it happens through a slow process of daily growth. Goals are usually accomplished by breaking them down into bite-size pieces and tackling them one at a time, step by step.

> **"If God simply handed us everything we want,**
> **He'd be taking from us our greatest prize -**
> **the joy of accomplishment." Frank A. Clark**

Life is so busy; every day we need to be reminded of what is really important. We all need accountability and encouragement. That is what this journal is intended to accomplish for you. Putting your goals and struggles down on paper will motivate you to take a serious look at the progress you are making in your walk with God. There is tremendous power generated by doing something on a daily basis, both physically and spiritually. Spending time daily with God brings about incredible long-term growth.

Whether you are a new Christian or a "veteran", this journal will help you establish or re-establish the basics of being close to God and being used by Him. Sometimes a fresh perspective can make all the difference. Each of the ten Steps is divided into four weeks of Bible study, prayer and thought-provoking, soul-searching questions. Each day, you will read a verse, think about what it means, and apply it to your own life. Be sure to pray over it.

In Step 1, you will examine and establish your relationship with God as your Father. In Step 2, you will discover what needs to change in your emotional and physical condition. Step 3 will help you improve your self-image and clarify your purpose in life. Step 4 is an evaluation of your gifts and abilities. In Step 5, you will become aware of the needs of others.

Throughout Step 6, you will work on reaching out to others. After Step 7, you will understand how to recognize God's voice. Step 8 emphasizes obeying the direction you receive from God. In Step 9, you will learn how self-discipline and spiritual habits will enable you to work for God effectively. Finally, in Step 10, you will explore how to become friends with God.

You CAN receive the promises God has made to you! With His help, you can make the change from incapacity to involvement; from futility to fulfillment; from potential to productivity. My prayer is that as you use this journal, every area of your life will be transformed.

Anything that you place in God's hands becomes better; He improves everything He touches. Just as a baby spends 40 weeks in the womb before making an entrance into the world, may these 40 weeks birth the spiritual life you have been hungering for!

**Liane R. Grant**

# CONTENTS: Weekly Goals

| | |
|---|---|
| **Step 1** | **Establishing Your Relationship with God** |
| Week 1 | Understand that God is your Father and you are His child. |
| Week 2 | Accept your father's human weaknesses, and realize that God is a perfect Father. |
| Week 3 | Realize and appreciate the gifts that your Heavenly Father gives you. |
| Week 4 | Learn how to demonstrate your love for God by giving to Him, with a good attitude. |
| | |
| **Step 2** | **Making Changes in Your Life** |
| Week 5 | Remove any barriers of sin that are standing between you and God. |
| Week 6 | Admit your emotional wounds to God, and allow Him to start the healing process. |
| Week 7 | Realize that attitudes are spirits; replace the negative ones in your life with positive ones. |
| Week 8 | Recognize any bad habits you have developed, and replace them with good habits. |
| | |
| **Step 3** | **Discovering your Identity and Calling** |
| Week 9 | Realize that as a child of the King of kings, you are royalty. |
| Week 10 | Accept the way God made you, and try to become more like Him, not like other people. |
| Week 11 | Become aware of the people in your circle of influence, and of your responsibility to them. |
| Week 12 | Recognize the burdens and desires God has given you — your calling. |

| **Step 4** | **Evaluating your Gifts and Abilities** |
|---|---|
| Week 13 | Recognize your natural abilities — things you are able to do effortlessly. |
| Week 14 | Identify the talents you have trained, and the talents you have buried. |
| Week 15 | Realize that some skills God asks you to develop will require courage and perseverance. |
| Week 16 | Understand how the gifts of the Spirit operate. |

| **Step 5** | **Becoming Aware of Needs** |
|---|---|
| Week 17 | Learn how to recognize your own needs. |
| Week 18 | Pay attention to the physical needs of those around you. |
| Week 19 | Become aware of the emotional needs of those around you. |
| Week 20 | Be conscious of the spiritual needs of those around you. |

| **Step 6** | **Reaching out to Others** |
|---|---|
| Week 21 | Understand your responsibility to pray for others. |
| Week 22 | Become aware of how you can minister to those in your circle of influence. |
| Week 23 | Realize the value of being involved in a ministry in your local church. |
| Week 24 | Discover the importance of teaching God's Word to others. |

| | |
|---|---|
| <u>**Step 7**</u> | <u>**Recognizing God's Voice**</u> |
| Week 25 | Learn to recognize how God speaks to you through the Bible. |
| Week 26 | Understand how God speaks to you through preaching and teaching. |
| Week 27 | Discover how God can speak to you through the words of another person. |
| Week 28 | Understand how to hear God speaking to your heart directly. |
| | |
| <u>**Step 8**</u> | <u>**Obeying God's Direction**</u> |
| Week 29 | Focus on obeying God as He shows you things in His Word. |
| Week 30 | Realize the importance of submission to those God has placed over you. |
| Week 31 | Learn how to be led of the Spirit in your daily life. |
| Week 32 | Decide to have a proper attitude in obeying God. |
| | |
| <u>**Step 9**</u> | <u>**Developing Self-Disicpline**</u> |
| Week 33 | Learn to discipline yourself to pray and fast. |
| Week 34 | Understand the importance of regular Bible study. |
| Week 35 | Discipline yourself to be a good steward of what God has given you. |
| Week 36 | Realize the importance of holiness in your lifestyle. |

| | |
|---|---|
| **<u>Step 10</u>** | **<u>Becoming Friends with God</u>** |
| Week 37 | Understand the importance of spending time with God. |
| Week 38 | Develop your communication with God. |
| Week 39 | Realize the importance of trust in your relationship with God. |
| Week 40 | Discover the importance of loyalty in your relationship with God. |

# ORDER MY STEPS
# Devotional Journal

# STEP 1:
## Establishing your
## Relationship with God

# STEP 1: *Establishing your Relationship with God*

Before you start this section, take a few minutes to evaluate your life right now. Each month, you can repeat this process to see how you are progressing in your walk with God. It is easy to overlook growth on a daily basis, but looking back over a whole month will help you see changes.

In this first step, you will focus on your Father-child relationship with God. You probably understand how a mother can love her child just because the child is hers. An infant cannot do anything for a parent; the parent does everything for them. After a long process of growth, the child is able to do much more. Parents love their children because of who they are, not what they do. Do you realize that God loves you for the same reason — because of who you are, not because of what you can do? He loves you because you are His child — all the reason He needs!

| Area of your life to evaluate: | Weak, Good or Great |
| --- | --- |
| Relationship with God as your Father | ✓ |
| Emotional and physical condition | ✓ |
| Self-image and purpose in life | ✓ |
| Development of gifts and abilities | ✓ |
| Awareness of others' needs | ✓ |
| Reaching out to others | ✓ |
| Recognizing God's voice | ✓ |
| Obeying God's direction | ✓ |
| Self-discipline and spiritual habits | ✓ |
| Relationship with God as your friend | ✓ |

You have started a journey to closeness with God, and usefulness in His kingdom. It only gets better from here!

## STEP 1: Establishing your Relationship with God
### Week 1 — Dates: 7/27–8/2

### This Week's Goal:
*Understand that God is your Father
and you are His child.*

### This Week's Verse:
*"Wherefore come out from among them, and be ye separate,
saith the Lord, and touch not the unclean thing; and I will
receive you, And will be a Father unto you, and ye shall be
my sons and daughters, saith the Lord Almighty."*
*2 Corinthians 6:17-18*

Why not start at the very beginning — by taking a close look at your relationship with God? Throughout the Bible, we find that God is many different things to us. He's the Alpha and Omega, the beginning and the ending, and everything in between.

However, repeatedly, God expresses His desire to be our Father. In fact, God is referred to as "Father" over 200 times in the New Testament! Entering into a Father-child relationship with the Lord is foundational to our spiritual growth.

| Prayer Requests | Answers to Prayer | Thanksgiving and Praise |
|---|---|---|
| | | |
| | | |
| | | |
| | | |
| | | |
| | | |
| | | |

# WEEK #1: Monday, 7/27

*"Wherefore come out from among them, and be ye separate, saith the Lord, and touch not the unclean thing; and I will receive you, And will be a Father unto you, and ye shall be my sons and daughters, saith the Lord Almighty."*
*2 Corinthians 6:17-18*

**Thought:** When you set yourself apart for God instead of following the crowd, He promises that He will become your Father, and you will become His child.

**Question:** How do you feel about God being your Father, and you being His child?

*So good to know that I have a Father that can supply every need I have. He is also my healer and He answers all my prayers (true. if it is wait, no, yes, etc.) My earthly father loved his children but there was never any emotional or physical affection shown to us.*

# WEEK #1: Tuesday, 7/28

*"A father of the fatherless, and a judge of the widows, is God in his holy habitation. God setteth the solitary in families: he bringeth out those which are bound with chains: but the rebellious dwell in a dry land."* *Psalm 68:5-6*

**Thought:** God will be a Father to you even if your own father is not around. He does not want you to be lonely; He wants you to be part of His family.

**Question:** Can you remember a time in your life when you needed your father, but for some reason he was not there? Did you turn to God for comfort instead?

*I did not know God as my Saviour when I was growing up. I'm glad I know Him now*

## WEEK #1: Wednesday, _7/29/_

*"For ye are all the children of God by faith in
Christ Jesus. For as many of you as have been
baptized into Christ have put on Christ."*
Galatians 3:26-27

**Thought:** When you act on your faith and are baptized, you
become a child of God, because you have taken on His name.

**Question:** How did you feel after you were baptized? Was it
easier to feel like you belonged to God?

_I felt clear and yes, I felt like
I belonged to God. I just didn't
know the seriousness of the H.S. in my
life til a few years later, but I'm
so glad that I do now._

## WEEK #1: Thursday, _____

*"But as many as received him, to them gave he power
to become the sons of God, even to them that believe on
his name: Which were born, not of blood, nor of the
will of the flesh, nor of the will of man, but of God."*
John 1:12-13

**Thought:** If you believe God and receive His Spirit, He will
give you everything you need to be His child.

**Question:** What changes did receiving the Holy Spirit make
in your perception of God? How did God help you to relate
to Him as a Father?

15

# WEEK #1: Friday, _7/31_

*"For ye have not received the spirit of bondage*
*again to fear; but ye have received the Spirit of*
*adoption, whereby we cry, Abba, Father."*
Romans 8:15

**Thought:** When the Holy Spirit is active in your life, you are constantly reminded that you are a child of God.

**Question:** Is the Holy Spirit currently active in your life ? What evidence can others see of this?

_I try to live my life so others_
_might see Jesus in me_

# WEEK #1: Saturday, _8/1/20_

*"For unto us a child is born, unto us a son is given:*
*and the government shall be upon his shoulder: and his*
*name shall be called Wonderful, Counsellor, The mighty*
*God, The everlasting Father, The Prince of Peace."*
Isaiah 9:6

**Thought:** God is your everlasting Father; He will never stop being a Father to you.

**Question:** Has your own father died, or have you ever worried about him dying? Do you realize that you never have to worry about God ceasing to be your Father?

_I'm so thankful that God is_
_always with me, it promises never to_
_leave me or forsake me_

## WEEK #1: Sunday, _8/2/20_

*"Behold, what manner of love the Father hath bestowed upon us, that we should be called the sons of God: therefore the world knoweth us not, because it knew him not."*
1 John 3:1

**Thought:** There is no love that can compare with the love God showed when He chose you to be His child.

**Question:** How much do you think God loves you?

_More than I could ever comprehend_

## WEEK #1: REVIEW

### This Week's Goal:
*Understand that God is your Father and you are His child.*

### This Week's Verse:
*"Wherefore come out from among them, and be ye separate, saith the Lord, and touch not the unclean thing; and I will receive you, And will be a Father unto you, and ye shall be my sons and daughters, saith the Lord Almighty."*
2 Corinthians 6:17-18

**Question:** How has your perspective changed this week? Have you learned anything new about your relationship with God? Do you feel comfortable with the thought of God being your Father, and you being His child?

_I am very comfortable with_
_Knowing God is my Father_

## STEP 1: Establishing your Relationship with God
### Week 2 — Dates: _____

**This Week's Goal:**
*Accept your father's human weaknesses,*
*and realize that God is a perfect Father.*

**This Week's Verse:**
*"If ye then, being evil, know how to give good gifts unto*
*your children, how much more shall your Father which is*
*in heaven give good things to them that ask him?"*
Matthew 7:11

Now that you understand your Father-child relationship with God, you may find it helpful to examine your feelings about your own father, since they can affect how you see God. No earthly father is perfect. Although your father probably loved you, he may have had difficulty showing that love to you in a way you could understand.

If you had difficulty trusting your father, you will have to deal with those feelings before you can completely trust God. Once you come to terms with your father's human weakness, you will be free to accept God as the perfect Heavenly Father, who loves you unconditionally just because you belong to Him.

| Prayer Requests | Answers to Prayer | Thanksgiving and Praise |
|---|---|---|
|  |  |  |
|  |  |  |
|  |  |  |
|  |  |  |
|  |  |  |
|  |  |  |
|  |  |  |

## WEEK #2: Monday, _____

*"If ye then, being evil, know how to give good gifts unto your children, how much more shall your Father which is in heaven give good things to them that ask him?"*
Matthew 7:11

**Thought:** Your father probably tried to do some good things for you, even though he was limited by his humanity. Imagine how much more God is able to bless you!

**Question:** What are some of the good things your father did for you?

_provided for us_
_disciplined us_
_____
_____
_____

## WEEK #2: Tuesday, _____

*"According as he hath chosen us in him before the foundation of the world, that we should be holy and without blame before him in love: Having predestinated us unto the adoption of children by Jesus Christ to himself, according to the good pleasure of his will,"*
Ephesians 1:4-5

**Thought:** No matter what your earthly family situation was, God intentionally chose you to be part of His family, because He wanted you to belong to Him.

**Question:** Did your father make you feel like you were wanted and needed in your family?

_____
_____
_____
_____
_____

## WEEK #2: Wednesday, _____

*"Furthermore we have had fathers of our flesh which corrected us, and we gave them reverence: shall we not much rather be in subjection unto the Father of spirits, and live? For they verily for a few days chastened us after their own pleasure; but he for our profit, that we might be partakers of his holiness."* Hebrews 12:9-10

**Thought:** Your father may have disciplined you at times for selfish reasons. God's discipline is always intended to make you a better person.

**Question:** How and why did your father discipline you as a child?

_____
_____
_____
_____


## WEEK #2: Thursday, _____

*"And he arose, and came to his father. But when he was yet a great way off, his father saw him, and had compassion, and ran, and fell on his neck, and kissed him."* Luke 15:20

**Thought:** Like the prodigal son, if you have distanced yourself from God, He will come running to meet you when you return, even if others are unforgiving.

**Question:** Can you recall a time when you rebelled and took the wrong path? How quick was your father to forgive you when you realized your mistake?

_____
_____
_____
_____
_____
_____

## WEEK #2: Friday, _____

*"The father of the righteous shall greatly rejoice: and he that begetteth a wise child shall have joy of him. Thy father and thy mother shall be glad, and she that bare thee shall rejoice."*
Proverbs 23:24-25

**Thought:** Your father may have shown pleasure in you only when you behaved. You may not have felt unconditional love from him, but you can feel it from God.

**Question:** Was your father hard to please? Did you ever feel like you were a disappointment to him?

_____

_____

_____

_____

_____

_____

## WEEK #2: Saturday, _____

*"When my father and my mother forsake me, then the LORD will take me up."*
Psalm 27:10

**Thought:** There may have been times in your life when you felt like your father let you down, but God was there wanting to help you.

**Question:** Did you ever feel physically or emotionally abandoned by your father? How did you deal with it — by turning to God or by getting bitter?

_____

_____

_____

_____

_____

_____

_"For if ye forgive men their trespasses, your heavenly Father will also forgive you: But if ye forgive not men their trespasses, neither will your Father forgive your trespasses."_
Matthew 6:14-15

**Thought:** Forgiving your father for his mistakes and imperfections will allow you to be forgiven by God for your mistakes and imperfections.

**Question:** Is there anything you can think of that you feel resentful toward your father about?

_____

_____

_____

_____

## WEEK #2: REVIEW

### This Week's Goal:
_Accept your father's human weaknesses, and realize that God is a perfect Father._

### This Week's Verse:
_If ye then, being evil, know how to give good gifts unto your children, how much more shall your Father which is in heaven give good things to them that ask him?"_
_Matthew 7:11_

**Question:** How has your perspective changed this week? Have you discovered any issues regarding your father that you had not yet dealt with? Have you been able to forgive your father and accept his humanity? Do you understand now that God is a perfect Father?

_____

_____

_____

_____

_____

## STEP 1: Establishing your Relationship with God
### Week 3 — Dates: _____

### This Week's Goal:
*Realize and appreciate the gifts that
your Heavenly Father gives you.*

### This Week's Verse:
*"Every good gift and every perfect gift is from above,
and cometh down from the Father of lights, with whom
is no variableness, neither shadow of turning."*
James 1:17

Now that you have accepted God as your perfect Heavenly Father who loves you unconditionally, you can take a look at the gifts He gives you. God gives you many blessings, in different forms and for different purposes.

Some of His gifts are intended to encourage and strengthen you; others are just to show you how much He loves you. Then, there are gifts that correct and direct you; to keep you on the right path. You need to appreciate all of God's gifts, even the ones that do not feel comfortable or welcome at the time!

| Prayer Requests | Answers to Prayer | Thanksgiving and Praise |
|---|---|---|
| | | |
| | | |
| | | |
| | | |
| | | |
| | | |
| | | |

**WEEK #3: Monday, _____**

*"Every good gift and every perfect gift is from above,
and cometh down from the Father of lights, with whom
is no variableness, neither shadow of turning."*
James 1:17

**Thought:** Every good thing in your life can be traced back to your Heavenly Father.

**Question:** What are some of the gifts and blessings that the Lord has given you?

_____
_____
_____
_____
_____
_____

**WEEK #3: Tuesday, _____**

*"And because ye are sons, God hath sent forth the
Spirit of his Son into your hearts, crying, Abba, Father.
Wherefore thou art no more a servant, but a son; and
if a son, then an heir of God through Christ."*
Galatians 4:6-7

**Thought:** One of the reasons God placed His Spirit inside your heart was to help you feel connected to Him as a Father.

**Question:** Has there ever been a season of prayerlessness in your life? Did you feel close to God during this time?

_____
_____
_____
_____
_____
_____

## WEEK #3: Wednesday, _____

*"And hope maketh not ashamed; because the
love of God is shed abroad in our hearts by the
Holy Ghost which is given unto us."*
Romans 5:5

**Thought:** God's Spirit inside you is a constant reminder of His love for you.

**Question:** When you feel God's Spirit, do you also feel God's love in a strong and powerful way?

_____

_____

_____

_____

_____


## WEEK #3: Thursday, _____

*"...for your Father knoweth what things
ye have need of, before ye ask him."*
Matthew 6:8

*"But my God shall supply all your need according
to his riches in glory by Christ Jesus."*
Philippians 4:19

**Thought:** God knows exactly what you need, and has promised to supply it. Also, at times He will bless you with something you desire, but do not really need.

**Question:** Do you have a difficult time differentiating between your desires and your needs?

_____

_____

_____

_____

_____

## WEEK #3: Friday, _____

*"Finally, my brethren, be strong in the Lord, and in the power of his might. Put on the whole armour of God, that ye may be able to stand against the wiles of the devil."*
Ephesians 6:10-11

**Thought:** One of the gifts God gives you is protection from the enemy. In order to have this protection, you must put on the armour that He has provided.

**Question:** Can you think of a time when God has protected you from danger, from evil or from making a serious mistake?

_____
_____
_____
_____


## WEEK #3: Saturday, _____

*"For whom the LORD loveth he correcteth; even as a father the son in whom he delighteth."* Proverbs 3:12

*"Behold, happy is the man whom God correcteth: therefore despise not thou the chastening of the Almighty:"* Job 5:17

**Thought:** There will be times when God's love will require that He correct you. It will be much less painful if you accept His correction instead of resisting it.

**Question:** Can you recall a time when you did something wrong and God had to correct you? How did you respond — by learning the lesson or by getting angry?

_____
_____
_____
_____
_____
_____

*"Howbeit when he, the Spirit of truth, is come, he will guide you into all truth..."* John 16:13

*"For as many as are led by the Spirit of God, they are the sons of God."* Romans 8:14

**Thought:** Another reason God gave you His Spirit is to lead you. If you are truly His child, you will follow the leading of His Spirit.

**Question:** When have you had better results in making decisions — when you followed your own instincts or when you asked God to lead you?

_____

_____

_____

_____

## WEEK #3: REVIEW

### This Week's Goal:
*Realize and appreciate the gifts that your Heavenly Father gives you.*

### This Week's Verse:
*"Every good gift and every perfect gift is from above, and cometh down from the Father of lights, with whom is no variableness, neither shadow of turning.*
James 1:17

**Question:** This week, have you learned about any of God's gifts that you were not aware of before? Do you feel like you appreciate His gifts more now?

_____

_____

_____

_____

## STEP 1: Establishing your Relationship with God
### Week 4 — Dates: _____

### This Week's Goal:
*Learn how to demonstrate your love for God
by giving to Him, with a good attitude.*

### This Week's Verses:
*"Blessed be the Lord, who daily loadeth us with
benefits, even the God of our salvation. Selah."*
Psalm 68:19

*"What shall I render unto the LORD
for all his benefits toward me?"*
Psalm 116:12

Now that you are aware of the gifts your Heavenly Father gives you, you can focus on what you can give to Him. Every relationship must be a two-way relationship in order to survive. Giving to God will not only show your love for Him, but will actually deepen that love, and enable you to serve Him more effectively. Jesus said in John 8:29 that He did always those things that pleased the Father. Since you are trying to be more like Jesus, your goal each day should be to live, act and speak in a way that brings pleasure to your Heavenly Father.

| Prayer Requests | Answers to Prayer | Thanksgiving and Praise |
|---|---|---|
| | | |
| | | |
| | | |
| | | |
| | | |
| | | |
| | | |

**WEEK #4: Monday, _____**

*"Blessed be the Lord, who daily loadeth us with*
*benefits, even the God of our salvation. Selah."*
Psalm 68:19

*"What shall I render unto the LORD*
*for all his benefits toward me?"*
Psalm 116:12

**Thought:** If you were to stop and try to count the blessings God has given you, you would be overwhelmed. Your natural response is to want to give back to Him.

**Question:** How has God blessed you? How have you tried to express your thankfulness to Him for His blessings?

_____

_____

_____

_____

_____


**WEEK #4: Tuesday, _____**

*"And thou shalt love the LORD thy God with all thine*
*heart, and with all thy soul, and with all thy might."*
Deuteronomy 6:5

**Thought:** The most important way you can give to God is by loving Him completely and unreservedly.

**Question:** How are you loving God with all your heart? With all your soul? With all your might?

_____

_____

_____

_____

_____

## WEEK #4: Wednesday, _____

*"But now, O LORD, thou art our father; we are the clay, and thou our potter; and we all are the work of thy hand."*
Isaiah 64:8

**Thought:** You can give submission and obedience to God by picturing yourself as a clay vessel being molded and shaped by His hands.

**Question:** How are you allowing God to shape your life?

_____
_____
_____
_____
_____
_____

## WEEK #4: Thursday, _____

*"But the hour cometh, and now is, when the true worshippers shall worship the Father in spirit and in truth: for the Father seeketh such to worship him. God is a Spirit: and they that worship him must worship him in spirit and in truth."*
John 4:23-24

**Thought:** Worship is a beautiful thing you can give to the Lord. He is actually looking for people who will worship Him.

**Question:** Do you find it difficult to worship God? Do you do it anyway?

_____
_____
_____
_____
_____
_____
_____

## WEEK #4: Friday, _____

*"For this God is our God for ever and ever:*
*he will be our guide even unto death."*
Psalm 48:14

**Thought:** Giving your trust to God involves realizing that your understanding is limited, and deciding to follow His directions instead of your own.

**Question:** How much do you trust the Lord? Is there any area of your life in which you don't trust Him, or that you try to hold back from Him?

_____

_____

_____

_____

_____

_____

## WEEK #4: Saturday, _____

*"Thou wilt shew me the path of life: in thy*
*presence is fulness of joy; at thy right hand*
*there are pleasures for evermore."*
Psalm 16:11

**Thought:** You can give to God by spending time with Him. He loves to have you in His presence!

**Question:** How much time do you spend with God, in prayer, worship and reading His Word? Do you find joy by being in His presence?

_____

_____

_____

_____

_____

_____

*"But this I say, He which soweth sparingly shall reap also sparingly; and he which soweth bountifully shall reap also bountifully. Every man according as he purposeth in his heart, so let him give; not grudgingly, or of necessity: for God loveth a cheerful giver."* 2 Corinthians 9:6-7

**Thought:** There are many different things we can give to God. The important thing is that we give generously and with a cheerful attitude.

**Question:** What type of attitude do you usually have when you give to God?

_____

_____

_____

_____

## WEEK #4: REVIEW

**This Week's Goal:**
*Learn how to demonstrate your love for God by giving to Him, with a good attitude.*

**This Week's Verse:**
*"Blessed be the Lord, who daily loadeth us with benefits, even the God of our salvation. Selah."* Psalm 68:19

*"What shall I render unto the LORD for all his benefits toward me?"* Psalm 116:12

**Question:** What have you learned about giving to God this week? Are you going to start giving Him something you were holding back before, and will you make some changes in your attitude?

_____

_____

_____

_____

# ORDER MY STEPS
## Devotional Journal

## STEP 2:
## Making Changes
## in your Life

## STEP 2: Making Changes in Your Life

Before you start this section, do another evaluation of your life. Compare it with the first evaluation you did, four weeks ago. Have there been some changes, particularly in the first area — concerning your relationship with God as Father? In this next step, you will be taking a look at some other changes you need to make in your life. According to Hebrews 12:1, we can run the race of life much easier when we lay aside the weights and sins that are hindering us. It is very difficult to serve God while dragging along a load of sin, emotional wounds, negative attitudes and bad habits.

Eliminating these things will lighten your load so that you can enjoy your walk with God and be more effective in your work for Him. Your human nature resists change, but your spiritual life depends and thrives on it! If you are not getting closer to God, you are getting farther from Him. In order to be a Christian ("Christ-like"), you must allow Jesus to shape your life to fit His pattern. Your personality may have to undergo some adjustments to match His!

| Area of your life to evaluate: | Weak, Good or Great |
|---|---|
| Relationship with God as your Father | |
| Emotional and physical condition | |
| Self-image and purpose in life | |
| Development of gifts and abilities | |
| Awareness of others' needs | |
| Reaching out to others | |
| Recognizing God's voice | |
| Obeying God's direction | |
| Self-discipline and spiritual habits | |
| Relationship with God as your friend | |

You are becoming a new creature in Christ; everything is changing!

## STEP 2: Making Changes in Your Life
## Week 5 — Dates: _____

### This Week's Goal:
*Remove any barriers of sin that are*
*standing between you and God.*

### This Week's Verse:
*"If I regard iniquity in my heart, the Lord will not hear me."*
Psalm 66:18

Have you ever felt like God was not even listening to your prayers, much less answering them? The psalmist David learned that when he had sin in his life and did not deal with it, God did not listen to him. The only prayer God can hear from someone in that situation is a prayer of repentance! This week, you will focus on removing any sins in your life that have become barriers between you and God. Repentance needs to be a daily action that we take to keep a close connection with God. When we allow even what seem like "little sins" to accumulate, it is very difficult to feel close to God.

| Prayer Requests | Answers to Prayer | Thanksgiving and Praise |
|---|---|---|
|  |  |  |
|  |  |  |
|  |  |  |
|  |  |  |
|  |  |  |
|  |  |  |
|  |  |  |

## WEEK #5: Monday, _____

*"If I regard iniquity in my heart, the Lord will not hear me."*
Psalm 66:18

**Thought:** If you know you have sin in your life and do not do anything about it, God will not hear your prayers.

**Question:** Is there any sin in your life that you have allowed to stay there?

_____
_____
_____
_____
_____
_____
_____
_____

## WEEK #5: Tuesday, _____

*"For godly sorrow worketh repentance to salvation not to be repented of: but the sorrow of the world worketh death."*
2 Corinthians 7:10

**Thought:** Conviction is the feeling God puts in your heart that says, "I should not do that".

**Question:** Do you recognize conviction when you feel it? Do you follow through on conviction by repenting?

_____
_____
_____
_____
_____
_____
_____

## WEEK #5: Wednesday, _____

*"If we say that we have no sin, we deceive ourselves, and the truth is not in us. If we confess our sins, he is faithful and just to forgive us our sins, and to cleanse us from all unrighteousness."* 1 John 1:8-9

**Thought:** If you will repent of your sin, you can count on the fact that God will forgive you and make you clean again.

**Question:** Are there any sins in your life for which you need to repent?

_____

_____

_____

_____

_____

## WEEK #5: Thursday, _____

*"Let no man say when he is tempted, I am tempted of God: for God cannot be tempted with evil, neither tempteth he any man: But every man is tempted, when he is drawn away of his own lust, and enticed. Then when lust hath conceived, it bringeth forth sin: and sin, when it is finished, bringeth forth death."*
James 1:13-15

**Thought:** You are tempted to sin when something appeals to your physical desires, and you allow yourself to think about it.

**Question:** What things seem to tempt you the most? What are your weak areas?

_____

_____

_____

_____

_____

## WEEK #5: Friday, _____

*"I will behave myself wisely in a perfect way. O when wilt thou come unto me? I will walk within my house with a perfect heart. I will set no wicked thing before mine eyes: I hate the work of them that turn aside; it shall not cleave to me."* Psalm 101:2-3

**Thought:** What you allow yourself to look at will have a direct influence on your thoughts, desires and actions.

**Question:** What do you allow into your mind through books, magazines and audio/visual media?

_____
_____
_____
_____


## WEEK #5: Saturday, _____

*"If a man therefore purge himself from these, he shall be a vessel unto honour, sanctified, and meet for the master's use, and prepared unto every good work. Flee also youthful lusts: but follow righteousness, faith, charity, peace, with them that call on the Lord out of a pure heart."*
2 Timothy 2:21-22

**Thought:** In order to be used by God, you need to put distance between you and the things that tempt you, and concentrate on good things.

**Question:** What specific things do you need to distance yourself from, in order to avoid temptation and be available for God to use?

_____
_____
_____
_____
_____

*"And have no fellowship with the unfruitful works of darkness, but rather reprove them. For it is a shame even to speak of those things which are done of them in secret. But all things that are reproved are made manifest by the light: for whatsoever doth make manifest is light."*
Ephesians 5:11-13

**Thought:** If you spend time with sinners, they will influence you negatively unless you have a strong positive influence.

**Question:** Are there any relationships that are having a negative effect on you? What changes should you make?

_____

_____

_____

_____

_____

## WEEK #5: REVIEW

### This Week's Goal:
*Remove any barriers of sin that are standing between you and God.*

### This Week's Verse:
*"If I regard iniquity in my heart, the Lord will not hear me:"*
Psalm 66:18

**Question:** What do you feel has been accomplished in your life this week, by taking a close (and maybe painful) look at your life? Do you feel like you have removed some things that were standing between you and God?

_____

_____

_____

_____

_____

## STEP 2: Making Changes in Your Life
### Week 6 — Dates: _____

### This Week's Goal:
*Admit your emotional wounds to God,*
*and allow Him to start the healing process.*

### This Week's Verse:
*"Seeing then that we have a great high priest, that is passed*
*into the heavens, Jesus the Son of God, let us hold fast our*
*profession. For we have not an high priest which cannot*
*be touched with the feeling of our infirmities; but was*
*in all points tempted like as we are, yet without sin."*
Hebrews 4:14-15

Have you ever been hurt emotionally? Very few people get through life without receiving some major emotional wounds. The critical thing is how you deal with these wounds. If you bury the hurt inside your heart, like a seed it will begin to grow. At some point you will have to pull out that plant, in order to survive spiritually. It is much easier to pull out a small weed than one that has been allowed the time to send down deep roots. Jesus understands your hurts, and is waiting for you to let Him start the healing process. You can get to the place where whenever you get hurt emotionally, you can immediately take it to Jesus, so that hurt never gets a chance to take root inside your heart.

| Prayer Requests | Answers to Prayer | Thanksgiving and Praise |
|---|---|---|
|  |  |  |
|  |  |  |
|  |  |  |
|  |  |  |
|  |  |  |
|  |  |  |
|  |  |  |

## WEEK #6: Monday, _____

*"Seeing then that we have a great high priest, that is passed into the heavens, Jesus the Son of God, let us hold fast our profession. For we have not an high priest which cannot be touched with the feeling of our infirmities; but was in all points tempted like as we are, yet without sin."*
Hebrews 4:14-15

**Thought:** In His life here on earth, Jesus experienced every painful emotion that you do. He understands exactly how you feel!

**Question:** Have you ever not prayed about emotional pain because you thought the Lord would not understand or care?

_____
_____
_____
_____
_____

## WEEK #6: Tuesday, _____

*"And God shall wipe away all tears from their eyes; and there shall be no more death, neither sorrow, nor crying, neither shall there be any more pain: for the former things are passed away."* Revelation 21:4

**Thought:** Until we get to heaven, we will feel pain when someone that we love dies. However, God promises to comfort you in your pain.

**Question:** Have you lost a loved one to death? Did you allow God to comfort you?

_____
_____
_____
_____
_____

## WEEK #6: Wednesday, _____

*"I looked on my right hand, and beheld, but there was no man that would know me: refuge failed me; no man cared for my soul. I cried unto thee, O LORD: I said, Thou art my refuge and my portion in the land of the living."*
Psalm 142:4-5

**Thought:** When it seems like you are all alone and nobody cares about you, it is time to focus your full attention on God and realize that He is always there!

**Question:** Have you ever felt completely alone? Did you turn to God for help?

_____

_____

_____

_____


## WEEK #6: Thursday, _____

*"He came unto his own, and his own received him not."*
John 1:11

*"He is despised and rejected of men; a man of sorrows, and acquainted with grief: and we hid as it were our faces from him; he was despised, and we esteemed him not."*
Isaiah 53:3

**Thought:** Jesus knew what it was like to be rejected, but He kept doing what was right in spite of it. He did not give up!

**Question:** Have you ever felt rejected? Did you withdraw into a shell, or did you keep on doing the things you knew God wanted you to do?

_____

_____

_____

_____

## WEEK #6: Friday, _____

*"But Jesus said unto him, Judas, betrayest*
*thou the Son of man with a kiss?"* Luke 22:48
*"Looking diligently lest any man fail of the grace of God;*
*lest any root of bitterness springing up trouble you,*
*and thereby many be defiled;"* Hebrews 12:15

**Thought:** Jesus knew the sting of betrayal, but continued loving in spite of it. The temptation to become bitter is never so strong as when we feel betrayed.

**Question:** Have you ever felt betrayed by someone you trusted? Did you allow yourself to become bitter, or did you go to Jesus, knowing He would understand?

_____
_____
_____
_____


## WEEK #6: Saturday, _____

*"There is therefore now no condemnation to them which*
*are in Christ Jesus, who walk not after the flesh, but after*
*the Spirit. For the law of the Spirit of life in Christ Jesus*
*hath made me free from the law of sin and death."*
Romans 8:1-2

**Thought:** Condemnation is a tool the devil uses to make you feel like you have failed miserably and there is no hope for you. God can set you free from this!

**Question:** Have you ever heard this: "You're no good; you can't live for God; you will never amount to anything"? Did you realize where it was coming from?

_____
_____
_____
_____

*"And ye shall know that I am in the midst of Israel,
and that I am the LORD your God, and none else:
and my people shall never be ashamed."*
Joel 2:27

**Thought:** God understands when you feel ashamed of
yourself, but He does not intend for you to keep feeling that
way!

**Question:** Have you ever felt horribly ashamed of something
you did? Were you able to get rid of the feeling yourself, or
did you need God's help?

_____
_____
_____
_____

## WEEK #6: REVIEW

**This Week's Goal:**
*Admit your emotional wounds to God,
and allow Him to start the healing process.*

**This Week's Verse:**
*"Seeing then that we have a great high priest, that is passed
into the heavens, Jesus the Son of God, let us hold fast our
profession. For we have not an high priest which cannot be
touched with the feeling of our infirmities; but was in all
points tempted like as we are, yet without sin."*
Hebrews 4:14-15

**Question:** This week, did you allow God to pull some "roots
of bitterness" out of your heart? Will you allow Him to
continue the healing process until it is complete?

_____
_____
_____
_____

## STEP 2: Making Changes in Your Life
Week 7 — Dates: _____

### This Week's Goal:
*Realize that attitudes are spirits; replace
the negative ones in your life with positive ones.*

### This Week's Verse:
*"Let all bitterness, and wrath, and anger, and clamour, and
evil speaking, be put away from you, with all malice: And be
ye kind one to another, tenderhearted, forgiving one another,
even as God for Christ's sake hath forgiven you."*
Ephesians 4:31-32

Attitudes — they can make or break your spiritual life!
Webster's dictionary defines both "attitude" and "spirit" as
a disposition (mood). Let's face it — bad attitudes are bad
spirits that try to influence your actions. They are like leeches
trying to attach themselves to you, and sometimes you may
need someone else to point them out to you. Good attitudes
are from the Lord, but a bad attitude grieves Him. If you are
full of the Holy Spirit, you have power available to you in
the name of Jesus to bind (disable) evil spirits. The next time
you feel a bad attitude coming on, deal with it in the name
of Jesus before it drains your spiritual life-blood! Ask God
to help you discern attitudes, so you can recognize bad ones
quickly. You do not have to be a slave to your moods!

| Prayer Requests | Answers to Prayer | Thanksgiving and Praise |
|---|---|---|
|  |  |  |
|  |  |  |
|  |  |  |
|  |  |  |
|  |  |  |
|  |  |  |
|  |  |  |

**WEEK #7: Monday, _____**

*"Let all bitterness, and wrath, and anger, and clamour,
and evil speaking, be put away from you, with all malice:
And be ye kind one to another, tenderhearted, forgiving one
another, even as God for Christ's sake hath forgiven you."*
Ephesians 4:31-32

**Thought:** God is grieved when you allow a bad attitude in your life. He wants you to get rid of it, and replace it with a good attitude.

**Question:** Have you ever felt a bad mood come on you unexpectedly and felt like you were helpless to do anything about it? Did you try binding it in Jesus' name?

_____
_____
_____
_____
_____

**WEEK #7: Tuesday, _____**

*"A new commandment I give unto you, That ye love one
another; as I have loved you, that ye also love one another."*
John 13:34

**Thought:** The main attitude God wants us to have is one of love. This is the opposite of feeling angry, vindictive and hateful.

**Question:** Do you have hateful feelings toward anyone? Try binding hate and loosing love in your life, and see what a difference it makes.

_____
_____
_____
_____
_____
_____

## WEEK #7: Wednesday, _____

*"Likewise, ye younger, submit yourselves unto the elder. Yea, all of you be subject one to another, and be clothed with humility: for God resisteth the proud, and giveth grace to the humble."*
1 Peter 5:5

**Thought:** In order to be on the same team as God, you must have a spirit of humility. You cannot be selfish, proud or rebellious, and expect God to approve.

**Question:** As you search your heart today, do you see any pride there? Say "no" to pride, and ask God to give you a humble spirit.

_____

_____

_____

_____

_____

## WEEK #7: Thursday, _____

*"But without faith it is impossible to please him: for he that cometh to God must believe that he is, and that he is a rewarder of them that diligently seek him."*
Hebrews 11:6

**Thought:** If you want to please God, you need faith in your life. There is no room for depression, discouragement or self-pity, which are enemies of faith.

**Question:** Have you ever fallen into a pit of depression? Did you grab hold of your faith and hang on until you got out?

_____

_____

_____

_____

_____

**WEEK #7: Friday, _____**

*"For God hath not given us the spirit of fear; but of power, and of love, and of a sound mind."* 2 Timothy 1:7

*"And the peace of God, which passeth all understanding, shall keep your hearts and minds through Christ Jesus."* Phliippians 4:7

**Thought:** God intends for you to have peace in your heart. He does not want you to feel fearful, confused or anxious.

**Question:** Have you ever felt fear come on you and hold you in a vice grip? Did you pray until the fear left and peace came?

_____
_____
_____
_____


**WEEK #7: Saturday, _____**

*"Therefore with joy shall ye draw water out of the wells of salvation."* Isaiah 12:3

*"... for this day is holy unto our Lord: neither be ye sorry; for the joy of the LORD is your strength."* Nehemiah 8:10

**Thought:** God plans for your life to be full of joy. He wants to protect you from a critical, unhappy and jealous spirit which would try to steal your joy.

**Question:** Are you a joyful person? Have you ever felt critical and negative, and had to make a decision not to keep that spirit around?

_____
_____
_____
_____

*"The soul of the sluggard desireth, and hath nothing: but the soul of the diligent shall be made fat."* Proverbs 13:4
*"Whatsoever thy hand findeth to do, do it with thy might;..."*
Ecclesiastes 9:10

**Thought:** Vibrant, alive Christians are motivated and full of purpose. Feeling lazy or apathetic is a danger signal.

**Question:** Have you ever felt a "Why bother?" attitude? Did you decide to leave that attitude behind and do your best at what you knew God wanted you to do?

_____

_____

_____

_____

## WEEK #7: REVIEW

### This Week's Goal:
*Realize that attitudes are spirits; replace the negative ones in your life with positive ones.*

### This Week's Verse:
*"Let all bitterness, and wrath, and anger, and clamour, and evil speaking, be put away from you, with all malice: And be ye kind one to another, tenderhearted, forgiving one another, even as God for Christ's sake hath forgiven you."*
Ephesians 4:31-32

**Question:** What have you learned about attitudes and spirits this week? Were you relieved to find out that you do not have to be the victim of a bad attitude, because you have the power to dispel it in Jesus' name?

_____

_____

_____

_____

## STEP 2: Making Changes in Your Life
### Week 8 — Dates: _____

### This Week's Goal:
*Recognize any bad habits you have developed,
and replace them with good habits.*

### This Week's Verses:
*"I will behave myself wisely in a perfect way...
I will walk within my house with a perfect heart."*
Psalm 101:2

*"In all things shewing thyself a pattern of good works..."*
Titus 2:7

Although you have dealt with wrong attitudes in your life, you may find that you still have some negative behaviour patterns as a result of those attitudes. Follow through on the victory over bad attitudes by cleaning up any bad habits. This will take time and discipline; research shows that it takes at least 30 days to form a new habit. Be patient, because you are on the right track! 2 Corinthians 10:5 tells us to cast down imaginations and bring our thoughts into captivity to the obedience of Christ. There may be habits you decide to get rid of which are not necessarily sinful, but are hindering you from being your best for God or from giving Him the time He deserves.

| Prayer Requests | Answers to Prayer | Thanksgiving and Praise |
|---|---|---|
| | | |
| | | |
| | | |
| | | |
| | | |
| | | |
| | | |

*"I will behave myself wisely in a perfect way...I will walk within my house with a perfect heart."* Psalm 101:2
*"In all things shewing thyself a pattern of good works..."*
Titus 2:7

**Thought:** God is concerned about the patterns or habits in your life. He intends for your behaviour to reflect your love for Him and your commitment to Him.

**Question:** Have you ever consciously worked on getting rid of a bad habit, or developing a new good habit? Are you ready to do it again, for God?

_____
_____
_____
_____

*"Know ye not, that to whom ye yield yourselves servants to obey, his servants ye are to whom ye obey; whether of sin unto death, or of obedience unto righteousness?"* Romans 6:16

*"All things are lawful unto me, but all things are not expedient: all things are lawful for me, but I will not be brought under the power of any."* 1 Corinthians 6:12

**Thought:** If there is anything in your life that holds power over you and that you cannot resist, then you are a slave to that thing. It will hinder your walk with God.

**Question:** Is there any food, drink, substance, activity or person that you are addicted to, and cannot seem to give up?

_____
_____
_____
_____

## WEEK #8: Wednesday, _____

*"Howbeit this kind goeth not out but by prayer and fasting."*
Matthew 17:21

*"But I keep under my body, and bring it into subjection:
lest that by any means, when I have preached to others,
I myself should be a castaway."* 1 Corinthians 9:27

**Thought:** In order to be used of God, you will need faith. According to Jesus, prayer and fasting are required to have mountain-moving faith.

**Question:** How disciplined are you in your eating habits? Can you say "no" to food when it is time to fast? Do you eat properly in order to stay healthy?

_____

_____

_____

_____

_____

## WEEK #8: Thursday, _____

*"He telleth the number of the stars; he calleth
them all by their names."* Psalm 147:4

**Thought:** God planned out the earth and the planets in a very organized fashion, so it would run smoothly. Since we are made in His image, is it possible that if our surroundings are chaotic and scattered, we are feeling that way inside?

**Question:** Do you have a problem with disorganization? Could you focus better on what God wants you to do if you were more organized?

_____

_____

_____

_____

**WEEK #8: Friday,** _____

_"Redeeming the time, because the days are
evil. Wherefore be ye not unwise, but
understanding what the will of the Lord is."_
Ephesians 5:16-17

**Thought:** God has given you a limited amount of time to
work for Him. He wants you to use it wisely, to do His will.

**Question:** How are your time management skills? Do you
think you could be more effective for God if you used your
time more wisely?

_____

_____

_____

_____

_____


**WEEK #8: Saturday,** _____

_"And withal they learn to be idle, wandering about from
house to house; and not only idle, but tattlers also and
busybodies, speaking things which they ought not."_
1 Timothy 5:13

**Thought:** God is not pleased with people who gossip and
meddle in other people's business. He has much more
important things for His children to do!

**Question:** Do you have a weakness for gossip? Do you think
your friendships would improve if you refused to gossip,
since your friends would know they could trust you not to
talk about them behind their backs?

_____

_____

_____

_____

_____

*"Humble yourselves therefore under the mighty hand of God, that he may exalt you in due time: Casting all your care upon him; for he careth for you."* 1 Peter 5:6-7

**Thought:** God desires for you to surrender all your personal rights to Him, and then there will be no need for you to worry about what might happen!

**Question:** Do you have a tendency to worry about things? Have you tried surrendering to God and letting Him take care of the future?

_____
_____
_____
_____

### WEEK #8: REVIEW

**This Week's Goal:**
*Recognize any bad habits you have developed, and replace them with good habits.*

**This Week's Verses:**
*"I will behave myself wisely in a perfect way... I will walk within my house with a perfect heart."*
Psalm 101:2

*"In all things shewing thyself a pattern of good works..."*
Titus 2:7

**Question:** This week, have you become aware of any bad habits you need to get rid of? When are you going to start? What new good habits are you going to develop to replace the old bad habits?

_____
_____
_____
_____

# ORDER MY STEPS
# Devotional Journal

## STEP 3:
Discovering your
Identity and Calling

## STEP 3: Discovering your Identity and Calling

It is time for another evaluation. Have you made progress, especially in your emotional and physical condition? In Step 3, you will discover your identity and your calling. Do you realize that as a child of the King of kings, you are royalty? Allow this revelation to bring confidence to your life, and watch the change it makes. Also, you will find out that trying to be anyone but yourself is a big hindrance to your usefulness in God's kingdom. God expects you to grow in the areas you can change, and to accept the things you cannot change.

God has placed you in this generation for a specific purpose. The roles that you fill and the people who are in your circle of influence are not by accident. When you consider the burdens and calling God has put in your heart, you can find out the purpose God has for your life. This step is exciting!

| Area of your life to evaluate: | Weak, Good or Great |
|---|---|
| Relationship with God as your Father | |
| Emotional and physical condition | |
| Self-image and purpose in life | |
| Development of gifts and abilities | |
| Awareness of others' needs | |
| Reaching out to others | |
| Recognizing God's voice | |
| Obeying God's direction | |
| Self-discipline and spiritual habits | |
| Relationship with God as your friend | |

You have started a journey to closeness with God. It only gets better from here!

## STEP 3: Discovering your Identity and Calling
### Week 9 — Dates: _____

### This Week's Goal:
*Realize that as a child of the*
*King of kings, you are royalty.*

### This Week's Verse:
*"But ye are a chosen generation, a royal priesthood,*
*an holy nation, a peculiar people; that ye should*
*shew forth the praises of him who hath called*
*you out of darkness into his marvellous light:"*
1 Peter 2:9

You are special! God has chosen you to be part of His family. You are different from the rest of the world; you stand out in the crowd because you belong to Jesus. People may think you are different, and that is the way it should be. You are a representative of God Almighty on the earth.

God has taken you out of the darkness of obscurity into the spotlight of royalty. You are a prince or a princess! Hold your head high, walk with confidence, and be proud to be a Christian. You are a privileged one!

| Prayer Requests | Answers to Prayer | Thanksgiving and Praise |
|---|---|---|
|  |  |  |
|  |  |  |
|  |  |  |
|  |  |  |
|  |  |  |
|  |  |  |
|  |  |  |

**WEEK #9: Monday, _____**

*"But ye are a chosen generation, a royal priesthood,*
*an holy nation, a peculiar people; that ye should*
*shew forth the praises of him who hath called*
*you out of darkness into his marvellous light:*
1 Peter 2:9

**Thought:** God wants you to understand just how special and extraordinary you are. He has chosen you and you have become royalty.

**Question:** Do you feel special to God? How do you feel about being royalty?

_____
_____
_____
_____
_____
_____

**WEEK #9: Tuesday, _____**

*"Now therefore, if ye will obey my voice indeed, and keep*
*my covenant, then ye shall be a peculiar treasure unto*
*me above all people: for all the earth is mine:"*
Exodus 19:5

**Thought:** God treasures you, because you have decided to obey Him and belong to Him.

**Question:** Do you realize how much God values you? Do you feel treasured?

_____
_____
_____
_____
_____
_____

**WEEK #9: Wednesday, _____**

*"But know that the LORD hath set apart him that is godly
for himself: the LORD will hear when I call unto him."*
Psalm 4:3

**Thought:** God has set you apart just for Him; He wants your full attention. Along with that comes the promise that when you talk to Him, He will be listening!

**Question:** Have you been giving God your full attention, or have you been expecting Him to share you with other things or people?

_____
_____
_____
_____
_____
_____
_____

**WEEK #9: Thursday, _____**

*"Ye are the light of the world. A city that
is set on an hill cannot be hid."*
Matthew 5:14

**Thought:** As the world gets worse, you will shine brighter and be more noticeable because of your commitment to God.

**Question:** How are you being a light to the people around you who do not know God? Can they see a difference in you?

_____
_____
_____
_____
_____
_____

## WEEK #9: Friday, _____

*"If ye be reproached for the name of Christ, happy are ye; for the spirit of glory and of God resteth upon you: on their part he is evil spoken of, but on your part he is glorified.. Yet if any man suffer as a Christian, let him not be ashamed; but let him glorify God on this behalf."*
1 Peter 4:14-16

**Thought:** People in important positions always get criticized. They have to just accept the fact that this comes along with the position.

**Question:** Have you ever been ridiculed for being a Christian? Did you let it bother you, or did you just rejoice that you had been chosen by God for this honour?

_____

_____

_____

_____

_____

## WEEK #9: Saturday, _____

*"Now then we are ambassadors for Christ, as though God did beseech you by us: we pray you in Christ's stead, be ye reconciled to God."*
2 Corinthians 5:20

**Thought:** God has trusted you with the responsibility of representing Him to your world. He speaks to people through you, in order to bring them to Him.

**Question:** How well do you represent the Lord to the people around you?

_____

_____

_____

_____

*"The Spirit itself beareth witness with our spirit, that we are the children of God: And if children, then heirs; heirs of God, and joint heirs with Christ; if so be that we suffer with him, that we may be also glorified together."*
Romans 8:16-17

**Thought:** As a royal child of God, you are an heir or heiress. God wants to pass blessings along to you.

**Question:** What blessings have you received as a result of being God's royal child?

_____
_____
_____
_____

## WEEK #9: REVIEW

### This Week's Goal:
*Realize that as a child of the King of kings, you are royalty.*

### This Week's Verse:
*"But ye are a chosen generation, a royal priesthood, an holy nation, a peculiar people; that ye should shew forth the praises of him who hath called you out of darkness into his marvellous light:"*
1 Peter 2:9

**Question:** How has your perspective changed this week? Are you more aware of the privileged position you have as a royal child of God? Has this raised the level of your confidence in working for God?

_____
_____
_____
_____
_____

## Week 10 — Dates: _____

### This Week's Goal:
*Accept the way God made you, and try to become more like Him, not like other people.*

### This Week's Verse:
*"I will praise thee; for I am fearfully and wonderfully made: marvellous are thy works; and that my soul knoweth right well."*
Psalm 139:14

Are you comfortable being yourself? God made each one of us unique; He did not use a cookie cutter. When you consider the thousands of flowers He created, and the fact that each snowflake is different, you will understand that God likes variety. He is pleased with your natural appearance and personality, because He planned you that way.

Comparing yourself to others is a recipe for disappointment and discouragement, and will stifle your work for God. You need to compare yourself only to Jesus, and try to be more like Him. Patterning your life after His image will enhance the beauty that He created in you.

| Prayer Requests | Answers to Prayer | Thanksgiving and Praise |
|---|---|---|
|  |  |  |
|  |  |  |
|  |  |  |
|  |  |  |
|  |  |  |
|  |  |  |
|  |  |  |

**WEEK #10: Monday,** _____

*"I will praise thee; for I am fearfully and*
*wonderfully made: marvellous are thy works;*
*and that my soul knoweth right well."*
Psalm 139:14

**Thought:** Your human life is a miracle only God could create.
He made the intricate parts of your body, mind and soul to
work and function together.

**Question:** Do you praise God every day for the miracle of
being alive?

_____
_____
_____
_____
_____


**WEEK #10: Tuesday,** _____

*"Before I formed thee in the belly I knew thee; and*
*before thou camest forth out of the womb I sanctified*
*thee, and I ordained thee a prophet unto the nations."*
Jeremiah 1:5

**Thought:** Before your life was even conceived, God had
already established His purpose for your life, and made you
in such a way that you could accomplish it.

**Question:** How do you feel about the fact that God had your
life in His hands before you were even conceived, and that
He has a plan for you to fulfill?

_____
_____
_____
_____
_____

*"For we are his workmanship, created in
Christ Jesus unto good works, which God hath
before ordained that we should walk in them."*
Ephesians 2:10

**Thought:** Not only does God have a general purpose for your life, He has specific things that He has planned for you to accomplish.

**Question:** Are you aware that God has certain things for you to do, that He has not asked anyone else to do?

_____
_____
_____
_____
_____
_____

*"Commit thy works unto the LORD,
and thy thoughts shall be established."*
Proverbs 16:3

**Thought:** God desires to actually guide each and every step you take. This will bring delight to both you and to God.

**Question:** Are you conscious of the fact that God wants to lead you in everything you do throughout each day? Do you let Him take the lead?

_____
_____
_____
_____
_____
_____

_"For we dare not make ourselves of the number, or compare ourselves with some that commend themselves: but they measuring themselves by themselves, and comparing themselves among themselves, are not wise."_
2 Corinthians 10:12

**Thought:** One of the most foolish things you can do is compare yourself to others. This is a recipe for disappointment and discouragement.

**Question:** Do you have a tendency to compare yourself to others: "If only I could be like...." Have you asked God to help you get over this?

_____
_____
_____
_____

_"But when ye pray, use not vain repetitions, as the heathen do: for they think that they shall be heard for their much speaking. Be not ye therefore like unto them: for your Father knoweth what things ye have need of, before ye ask him."_
Matthew 6:7-8

**Thought:** God is not pleased when you try to pray like someone else. He wants your prayers to come straight from your heart to His, without any dressing up.

**Question:** Have you ever allowed your prayer life to be stifled by thinking you had to pray like someone else — the same posture, words or volume?

_____
_____
_____
_____

*"And lest I should be exalted above measure through
the abundance of the revelations, there was given
to me a thorn in the flesh, the messenger of Satan to
buffet me, lest I should be exalted above measure."*
2 Corinthians 12:7

**Thought:** Sometimes the things we want so badly for God to change in our lives are the things that are keeping us humble and useful.

**Question:** Is there anything in your life that bothers you, that you cannot change by yourself? Have you decided to do your best in spite of it, until God changes it?

_____

_____

_____

_____

## WEEK #10: REVIEW

### This Week's Goal:
*Accept the way God made you, and try to
become more like Him, not like other people.*

### This Week's Verse:
*"I will praise thee; for I am fearfully and
wonderfully made: marvellous are thy works;
and that my soul knoweth right well."*
Psalm 139:14

**Question:** What have you learned this week about God's unique plan for your life? Do you feel like you can now be content to be yourself? Have you stopped comparing yourself with other people?

_____

_____

_____

_____

## STEP 3: Discovering your Identity and Calling
### Week 11 — Dates: _____

### This Week's Goal:
*Become aware of the people in your circle of influence, and of your responsibility to them.*

This Week's Verse:
*"For if thou altogether holdest thy peace at this time, then shall there enlargement and deliverance arise to the Jews from another place; but thou and thy father's house shall be destroyed: and who knoweth whether thou art come to the kingdom for such a time as this?"*
Esther 4:14

Have you ever wondered why you are living in the twenty-first century? You are not here by accident; God has planned for you to live in this generation. Esther found herself in a position of importance and surrounded by royalty. Instead of relaxing and selfishly enjoying herself, she realized that God had placed her there for a specific purpose, which was to help others. There is a reason why you live where you do, work or attend school where you do, meet the people you do...it is all in the plan of God. This week you will become aware of the people in your circle of influence, and of your responsibility to them.

| Prayer Requests | Answers to Prayer | Thanksgiving and Praise |
|---|---|---|
|  |  |  |
|  |  |  |
|  |  |  |
|  |  |  |
|  |  |  |
|  |  |  |
|  |  |  |

## WEEK #11: Monday, _____

*"For if thou altogether holdest thy peace at this time, then shall there enlargement and deliverance arise to the Jews from another place; but thou and thy father's house shall be destroyed: and who knoweth whether thou art come to the kingdom for such a time as this?"*
Esther 4:14

**Thought:** Esther was born at exactly the right time, lived in exactly the right place, and did exactly the right thing to fulfill God's purpose in rescuing the Jews.

**Question:** Have you ever thought about why God has placed you where you are at this particular time? Are you aware that He has a purpose for you here and now?

_____
_____
_____
_____
_____


## WEEK #11: Tuesday, _____

*"For after this manner in the old time the holy women also, who trusted in God, adorned themselves, being in subjection unto their own husbands:"*
1 Peter 3:5

**Thought:** A wife has a responsibility to let her husband take the leadership of the home, and the husband's role is to protect her.

**Question:** If you are married, do you realize that God has a purpose for you in that marriage relationship?

_____
_____
_____
_____
_____

## WEEK #11: Wednesday, _____

*"And, ye fathers, provoke not your children to wrath: but bring them up in the nurture and admonition of the Lord."*
Ephesians 6:4

**Thought:** God's plan to pass the gospel on from generation to generation is carried out when parents teach their children about the ways of God.

**Question:** If you have children, are you aware of the purpose God has for your relationship with them? Are you teaching your children about God daily?

_____

_____

_____

_____

_____

## WEEK #11: Thursday, _____

*"Honour thy father and thy mother, as the LORD thy God hath commanded thee; that thy days may be prolonged, and that it may go well with thee, in the land which the LORD thy God giveth thee."*
Deuteronomy 5:16

**Thought:** God's promise to bless our lives depends on us respecting our parents.

**Question:** If your parents are still living, do you give them honour and respect, in your words and actions? Are you aware that God will bless you for this?

_____

_____

_____

_____

_____

_____

## WEEK #11: Friday, _____

*"And he answering said, Thou shalt love the Lord thy God with all thy heart, and with all thy soul, and with all thy strength, and with all thy mind; and thy neighbour as thyself."*
Luke 10:27

**Thought:** God intends for us to reach out to our neighbours. You live where you live for a purpose, not by accident.

**Question:** Do you know your neighbours' names? What else do you know about them? Have you attempted to become friends with them?

_____
_____
_____
_____
_____


## WEEK #11: Saturday, _____

*"How then shall they call on him in whom they have not believed? and how shall they believe in him of whom they have not heard? and how shall they hear without a preacher?"*
Romans 10:14

**Thought:** When you have a chance to tell someone about your relationship with God, it may be their only chance to hear about salvation.

**Question:** Do you share freely with people about your relationship with God? Do you keep in mind that it may be their only chance to hear about the opportunity of salvation?

_____
_____
_____
_____
_____
_____

**WEEK #11: Sunday, _____**

*"But if our gospel be hid, it is hid to them that are lost:"*
2 Corinthians 4:3

**Thought:** God never intended for us to hide the beautiful experience of salvation we have received. He meant for us to share it with others.

**Question:** Are you conscious of the souls of the people around you? Do you realize that if you do not tell them about Jesus, they may never hear the Gospel?

_____
_____
_____
_____

## WEEK #11: REVIEW

### This Week's Goal:
*Become aware of the people in your circle of influence, and of your responsibility to them.*

### This Week's Verse:
*"For if thou altogether holdest thy peace at this time, then shall there enlargement and deliverance arise to the Jews from another place; but thou and thy father's house shall be destroyed: and who knoweth whether thou art come to the kingdom for such a time as this?"*
Esther 4:14

**Question:** What changes have taken place this week in your concepts about others? Are you more aware of the people you have an opportunity to influence? Did you discover some people to whom you need to give more attention?

_____
_____
_____
_____
_____

## STEP 3: Discovering your Identity and Calling
## Week 12 — Dates: _____

### This Week's Goal:
*Recognize the burdens and desires*
*God has given you — your calling.*

### This Week's Verse:
*"Wherefore also we pray always for you, that our God*
*would count you worthy of this calling, and fulfil all*
*the good pleasure of his goodness, and the work of faith*
*with power: That the name of our Lord Jesus Christ may*
*be glorified in you, and ye in him, according to the grace*
*of our God and the Lord Jesus Christ."*
2 Thessalonians 1:11-12

God has a special "calling" or purpose for your life; a plan that He wants to fulfill through you. This week, you will do some soul-searching to get a clear picture of what God has shown you that He wants you to do. He probably has not told you everything yet — He expects you to walk by faith. However, you will probably discover that He has at least given you a hint, or a starting point. If you will take a step forward, you will find that He will direct each step after that.

| Prayer Requests | Answers to Prayer | Thanksgiving and Praise |
|---|---|---|
|  |  |  |
|  |  |  |
|  |  |  |
|  |  |  |
|  |  |  |
|  |  |  |
|  |  |  |

_"Wherefore also we pray always for you, that our God would count you worthy of this calling, and fulfil all the good pleasure of his goodness, and the work of faith with power: That the name of our Lord Jesus Christ may be glorified in you, and ye in him, according to the grace of our God and the Lord Jesus Christ."_
2 Thessalonians 1:11-12

**Thought:** God has a special purpose for your life; a work that He has planned for you to do. This is your calling.

**Question:** Do you want to know what your calling is? Are you willing to obey God by walking in that direction once He reveals it to you?

_____

_____

_____

_____

_____

_____

**WEEK #12: Tuesday,** _____

_"For the gifts and calling of God are without repentance."_
Romans 11:29

**Thought:** God is not going to ask you to do something, and then change His mind or take back your calling from you.

**Question:** Do you believe that God is serious about what He has called you to do?

_____

_____

_____

_____

_____

_____

## WEEK #12: Wednesday, _____

*"But when he saw the multitudes, he was moved with compassion on them, because they fainted, and were scattered abroad, as sheep having no shepherd."*
Matthew 9:36

**Thought:** Your calling or burden is sometimes easier to recognize if you look at what causes you to feel compassion.

**Question:** What moves you with compassion, or makes you cry? Is there something you feel deeply and strongly about, that you want to see changed?

_____

_____

_____

_____

## WEEK #12: Thursday, _____

*"And it shall come to pass in the last days, saith God, I will pour out of my Spirit upon all flesh: and your sons and your daughters shall prophesy, and your young men shall see visions, and your old men shall dream dreams: And on my servants and on my handmaidens I will pour out in those days of my Spirit; and they shall prophesy:"* Acts 2:17-18

**Thought:** Sometimes God speaks to us through dreams, visions and prophecy. He also speaks through preaching and exhortation.

**Question:** Has God showed you what He wants you to do with your life? Was it through one of the ways mentioned above, or through another method?

_____

_____

_____

_____

_____

**WEEK #12: Friday, _____**

*"He staggered not at the promise of God
through unbelief; but was strong in faith, giving
gloryto God; And being fully persuaded that, what
he had promised, he was able also to perform."*
Romans 4:20-21

**Thought:** Abraham had enough faith to believe that God would do what He had promised, even though Abraham knew it was humanly impossible.

**Question:** Do you believe that God can accomplish what He has promised to accomplish through your life, no matter how difficult it seems?

_____
_____
_____
_____
_____

**WEEK #12: Saturday, _____**

*"The steps of a good man are ordered by
the LORD: and he delighteth in his way."*
Psalm 37:23

**Thought:** If will lift your foot to take a step, God will show you where to put it down and which direction to go.

**Question:** Are you ready and willing to start walking in the direction of God's promises and calling for your life? Will you start today?

_____
_____
_____
_____
_____
_____

## WEEK #12: Sunday, _____

*"Being confident of this very thing, that he*
*which hath begun a good work in you will*
*perform it until the day of Jesus Christ:"*
Philippians 1:6

**Thought:** God always finishes what He starts. When you allow Him to start fulfilling His calling in your life, He will be with you from start to finish.

**Question:** Are you confident that God is going to help you every step of the way, as you follow your calling?

_____
_____
_____
_____

## WEEK #12: REVIEW

### This Week's Goal:
*Recognize the burdens and desires*
*God has given you — your calling.*

### This Week's Verse:
*"Wherefore also we pray always for you, that our*
*God would count you worthy of this calling, and fulfil*
*all the good pleasure of his goodness, and the work of faith*
*with power: That the name of our Lord Jesus Christ may*
*be glorified in you, and ye in him, according to the grace*
*of our God and the Lord Jesus Christ."*
2 Thessalonians 1:11-12

**Question:** Are you aware of the direction God wants to take you; the calling that He has for you to fulfill in your life? Do you have the faith to take the first step and allow Him to lead you forward?

_____
_____
_____
_____

# ORDER MY STEPS
# Devotional Journal

## STEP 4:
## Evaluating your
## Gifts and Abilities

## STEP 4: Evaluating your Gifts and Abilities

It is again time to take inventory of your life. Check back to your last evaluation and see what progress you have made. Has there been an improvement in your self-image? Do you understand now how special you are to God, and that He has a purpose for your life?

This month, you are going to take a look at your gifts and abilities. Each person has a unique personality and possesses certain talents. God planned it this way, so that together we can be the body of Christ, without anything lacking.

Each of us is an important piece of the puzzle! You will be evaluating your life in four areas: natural abilities, trained talents, developed skills, and spiritual gifts. You will find out where you shine in each of these areas, and become more aware of how God wants to use you.

| Area of your life to evaluate: | Weak, Good or Great |
|---|---|
| Relationship with God as your Father | |
| Emotional and physical condition | |
| Self-image and purpose in life | |
| Development of gifts and abilities | |
| Awareness of others' needs | |
| Reaching out to others | |
| Recognizing God's voice | |
| Obeying God's direction | |
| Self-discipline and spiritual habits | |
| Relationship with God as your friend | |

God has blessed you with many gifts and abilities; it's up to you to discover and use them!

## STEP 4: Evaluating your Gifts and Abilities
## Week 13 — Dates: _____

### This Week's Goal:
*Recognize your natural abilities —*
*things you are able to do effortlessly.*

### This Week's Verse:
*"If any man speak, let him speak as the oracles of God; if any*
*man minister, let him do it as of the ability which God giveth:*
*that God in all things may be glorified through Jesus Christ, to*
*whom be praise and dominion for ever and ever. Amen."*
1 Peter 4:11

Each person is born with natural abilities — things that they
seem to be able to do effortlessly. No two people have the
same set of abilities; each is unique. In His foreknowledge,
God knew what abilities you would need to fulfil the purpose
He has determined for your life, and He made sure you had
them.

This week, you will learn to recognize your natural abilities
and see how you can use them in service to God. Instead
of admiring what others can do and feeling like you have
nothing to offer, you will learn to appreciate and activate
your natural abilities.

| Prayer Requests | Answers to Prayer | Thanksgiving and Praise |
|---|---|---|
| | | |
| | | |
| | | |
| | | |
| | | |
| | | |
| | | |

*"If any man speak, let him speak as the oracles of God; if any man minister, let him do it as of the ability which God giveth: that God in all things may be glorified through Jesus Christ, to whom be praise and dominion for ever and ever. Amen."*
1 Peter 4:11

**Thought:** Your natural abilities — the things you can do without hardly trying — are a gift from God.

**Question:** Are you conscious of thanking God for the natural abilities which He has given you?

_____
_____
_____
_____
_____

**WEEK #13: Tuesday, _____**

*"That the communication of thy faith may become effectual by the acknowledging of every good thing which is in you in Christ Jesus."*
Philemon 1:6

**Thought:** Each person has a way of communication that comes naturally to them. They find this is the easiest way to share their faith with someone else.

**Question:** How do you most easily communicate to others what you are feeling — through speaking, writing, actions, music, drawing, or some other method?

_____
_____
_____
_____
_____
_____

## WEEK #13: Wednesday, _____

*"By this shall all men know that ye are my
disciples, if ye have love one to another."*
John 13:35

**Thought:** People will know we are Christians by the love that
we show to others. Each person has a way of showing love
that comes naturally to them.

**Question:** What is the easiest and most natural way for you
to show love to someone — by hugging, helping, giving,
encouraging, spending time together, or some other way?

_____

_____

_____

_____

_____

## WEEK #13: Thursday, _____

*"Remember them which have the rule over you, who have
spoken unto you the word of God: whose faith follow,
considering the end of their conversation."*
Hebrews 13:7

**Thought:** We all have to follow the leadership of those in
authority, and our leaders have to follow God. Each of us
answers to someone.

**Question:** What do you find easier — leading or following?
Are you willing to let God decide when it is time for you to
lead and when it is time for you to follow?

_____

_____

_____

_____

_____

_"They helped every one his neighbour; and every one said to his brother, Be of good courage. So the carpenter encouraged the goldsmith, and he that smootheth with the hammer him that smote the anvil, saying, It is ready for the sodering: and he fastened it with nails, that it should not be moved."_
Isaiah 41:6-7

**Thought:** Great things are accomplished when people work together and encourage each other. Some people have the gift of encouragement.

**Question:** Do you know someone who is an inspiration to those around them — always encouraging and lifting people up? Is it you?

_____
_____
_____
_____
_____

_"Blessed are the peacemakers: for they shall be called the children of God."_
Matthew 5:9

**Thought:** Every home and church needs a peacemaker — someone who is able to resolve conflicts between people, and help everyone get along together.

**Question:** Are you a peacemaker? Do you know someone who is? Do you realize the value of a peacemaker?

_____
_____
_____
_____
_____

*"Having then gifts differing according to the grace that is given to us, whether prophecy...or ministry... or he that teacheth...or he that exhorteth...he that giveth...he that ruleth...he that sheweth mercy..."*
Romans 12:6-8

**Thought:** There are many different natural abilities. The important thing is not which ones we possess, but that we use them for God with a good attitude.

**Question:** Other than the ones studied this week, what other natural abilities do you have?

_____

_____

_____

_____

## WEEK #13: REVIEW

### This Week's Goal:
*Recognize your natural abilities —
things you are able to do effortlessly.*

### This Week's Verse:
*"If any man speak, let him speak as the oracles of God; if any man minister, let him do it as of the ability which God giveth: that God in all things may be glorified through Jesus Christ, to whom be praise and dominion for ever and ever. Amen."*
1 Peter 4:11

**Question:** This week, did you discover any natural abilities that you were not aware of before? Do you understand that God created each person different for a reason? Are you going to use your abilities for Him, with a good attitude?

_____

_____

_____

_____

## STEP 4: Evaluating your Gifts and Abilities
## Week 14 — Dates: _____

### This Week's Goal:
*Identify the talents you have trained,*
*and the talents you have buried.*

### This Week's Verse:
*"Then he that had received the five talents went and traded*
*with the same, and made them other five talents...Well done,*
*thou good and faithful servant: thou hast been faithful over a*
*few things, I will make thee ruler over many things..."*
Matthew 25:16, 21

Now that you are aware of your natural abilities, you will focus on trained talents — things that you were born with an ability to do, but required training and effort to hone and perfect these skills. You may have taken lessons or simply worked at developing these skills on your own.

Perhaps you will discover a talent that you had buried! If so, you need to dig it up and apply training so that it will grow and increase as God has planned. When He gives us a talent, He does not want us to sit on it or put it up on a shelf to look nice. His plan is for us to use and increase it.

| Prayer Requests | Answers to Prayer | Thanksgiving and Praise |
|---|---|---|
| | | |
| | | |
| | | |
| | | |
| | | |
| | | |
| | | |

## WEEK #14: Monday, _____

*"Then he that had received the five talents went and traded with the same, and made them other five talents...Well done, thou good and faithful servant: thou hast been faithful over a few things, I will make thee ruler over many things..."*
Matthew 25:16, 21

**Thought:** God gives us talents according to our ability. He knows exactly what we can do with what He gives us, and expects us to increase our talents.

**Question:** Do you understand that when God gives you a talent, He expects you to invest time, discipline and effort to develop and refine it?

_____
_____
_____
_____


## WEEK #14: Tuesday, _____

*"But this I say, He which soweth sparingly shall reap also sparingly; and he which soweth bountifully shall reap also bountifully."*
2 Corinthians 9:6

**Thought:** The law of the harvest is that you reap in proportion to how much you sowed. In the same way, our talents will yield in proportion to our effort.

**Question:** What talents did you begin developing when you were a child? Did you stick with them over a long period of time, and keep learning and improving?

_____
_____
_____
_____
_____

## WEEK #14: Wednesday, _____

*"All scripture is given by inspiration of God, and is profitable for doctrine, for reproof, for correction, for instruction in righteousness: That the man of God may be perfect, throughly furnished unto all good works."*
2 Timothy 3:16-17

**Thought:** Some talents are increased through studying, and learning more about how they work and how to use them.

**Question:** Which of your talents have required studying in order for you to develop them fully? Did you learn all you could?

_____
_____
_____
_____
_____
_____

## WEEK #14: Thursday, _____

*"Who will render to every man according to his deeds: To them who by patient continuance in well doing seek for glory and honour and immortality, eternal life:"*
Romans 2:6-7

**Thought:** Some talents are developed by using them over and over and over, until they become second nature.

**Question:** Which talents have you developed by using them on a regular basis — daily, weekly etc.?

_____
_____
_____
_____
_____
_____

**WEEK #14: Friday, _____**

*"A man's gift maketh room for him,*
*and bringeth him before great men."*
Proverbs 18:16

**Thought:** When someone invests time and energy to develop a talent, opportunities arise for them to use that talent.

**Question:** What opportunities has God allowed to come your way, to use a talent that you had spent time developing?

_____
_____
_____
_____
_____


**WEEK #14: Saturday, _____**

*"Then he which had received the one talent came and*
*said, Lord...I was afraid, and went and hid thy talent in*
*the earth...His lord answered and said unto him, Thou*
*wicked and slothful servant...Take therefore the talent*
*from him, and give it unto him which hath ten talents."*
Matthew 25:24-26, 28

**Thought:** God is not pleased when people waste the talents that He gave them. As the saying goes, "Use it or lose it!"

**Question:** Have you buried any of the talents God gave you? Why did you bury them — out of fear, laziness, busyness, disobedience or selfishness?

_____
_____
_____
_____
_____
_____
_____

*"...he had wasted his goods...What shall I do? for my lord taketh away from me the stewardship...So he called every one of his lord's debtors unto him...And the lord commended the unjust steward, because he had done wisely..."*
Luke 16:1-2,5, 8

**Thought:** Humans make mistakes, and God knows that. When a mistake is pointed out to us, God wants us to take action and do what we can to correct it.

**Question:** If you have been guilty of burying or wasting a talent God gave you, what can you do to correct it?

_____

_____

_____

_____

## WEEK #14: REVIEW

**This Week's Goal:**
*Identify the talents you have trained,
and the talents you have buried.*

**This Week's Verse:**
*"Then he that had received the five talents went and traded with the same, and made them other five talents...Well done, thou good and faithful servant: thou hast been faithful over a few things, I will make thee ruler over many things..."*
Matthew 25:16, 21

**Question:** What have you learned about talents this week? Did you dig up any buried ones? How do you feel now that you have yielded everything to God?

_____

_____

_____

_____

## STEP 4: Evaluating your Gifts and Abilities
### Week 15 — Dates: _____

**This Week's Goal:**
*Realize that some skills God asks you to
develop will require courage and perseverance.*

**This Week's Verse:**
*"And he said unto me, My grace is sufficient for thee: for
my strength is made perfect in weakness. Most gladly
therefore will I rather glory in my infirmities, that the
power of Christ may rest upon me."*
2 Corinthians 12:9

So far, you have considered your natural abilities and the talents which you have trained over time. The next area to look at are skills that do not come naturally to you, but you know God has asked you to develop. Growing in these areas requires stepping out of your comfort zone and depending completely on God for help.

As you stretch and struggle to develop these new skills, you will see God's power manifested in your life. There is great potential for ministry when you step into this area, since you know beyond a shadow of a doubt that you cannot do it by yourself. God alone will get the glory!

| Prayer Requests | Answers to Prayer | Thanksgiving and Praise |
|---|---|---|
|  |  |  |
|  |  |  |
|  |  |  |
|  |  |  |
|  |  |  |
|  |  |  |
|  |  |  |

## WEEK #15: Monday, _____

*"And he said unto me, My grace is sufficient for thee:
for my strength is made perfect in weakness. Most
gladly therefore will I rather glory in my infirmities,
that the power of Christ may rest upon me."*
2 Corinthians 12:9

**Thought:** Sometimes God will ask you to do something that you feel humanly incapable of. When He does this, He promises to provide the strength you need.

**Question:** Has God asked you to do something that you know you are not capable of doing? Have you stepped out in faith on His Word, knowing He will help you?

_____
_____
_____
_____

## WEEK #15: Tuesday, _____

*"Have not I commanded thee? Be strong and of a good
courage; be not afraid, neither be thou dismayed: for the
LORD thy God is with thee whithersoever thou goest."*
Joshua 1:9

**Thought:** Often fear paralyzes people from doing what God has asked them to do. It is important to remember that He gave the command, and He promises to be there with you all the way.

**Question:** Has fear ever kept you from doing what you knew God wanted you to do? How did you deal with it — by drawing strength from God's promises?

_____
_____
_____
_____

## WEEK #15: Wednesday, _____

*"Fight the good fight of faith, lay hold on eternal life, whereunto thou art also called, and hast professed a good profession before many witnesses."*
1 Timothy 6:12

**Thought:** There will be times when you will have to fight to hang on to your faith. Faith will keep you out of the clutches of fear.

**Question:** Can you recall a time when you stepped out to do what God said, and your faith started to falter? Did you grab hold of it and keep fighting?

_____
_____
_____
_____
_____


## WEEK #15: Thursday, _____

*"For a great door and effectual is opened unto me, and there are many adversaries."*
1 Corinthians 16:9

**Thought:** Sometimes God will open a door for you — an area in which you can be effective. That does not mean it will be smooth sailing; there will be opposition.

**Question:** Can you think of a door God opened for you, and when you walked through, you found that people or things tried to stop you from going there? Did you keep doing what God said anyway?

_____
_____
_____
_____
_____

**WEEK #15: Friday, _____**

*"And let us not be weary in well doing: for
in due season we shall reap, if we faint not."*
Galatians 6:9

**Thought:** There will be times when you will have to keep on
going even when you feel like giving up, because you know
for sure you are doing what God wants.

**Question:** Have you ever felt like giving up, even though you
knew you were doing God's will? Did you get fresh strength
from God and keep going?

_____

_____

_____

_____

_____


**WEEK #15: Saturday, _____**

*"And he spake a parable unto them to this end,
that men ought always to pray, and not to faint;"*
Luke 18:1

**Thought:** Developing a prayer life will probably not come
easily to you. It is one of those things that you may have to
struggle with, and there will be many hindrances. Do not
give up; you will not regret sticking with it!

**Question:** How has your prayer life developed? What did
you have to struggle with to make it a priority? Is God asking
you for a greater prayer commitment?

_____

_____

_____

_____

_____

_____

_"Blessed is the man that endureth temptation: for when he is tried, he shall receive the crown of life, which the Lord hath promised to them that love him."_
James 1:12

**Thought:** When you do what God asks you, even if it is difficult, many temptations will come to try to stop you. God sees your struggle, and will reward you for your faithfulness!

**Question:** What difficulties have you struggled through and kept doing what God asked? Is there anything God has asked you to do that you have not yet obeyed?

_____
_____
_____
_____

### WEEK #15: REVIEW

**This Week's Goal:**
_Realize that some skills God asks you to develop will require courage and perseverance._

**This Week's Verse:**
_"And he said unto me, My grace is sufficient for thee: for my strength is made perfect in weakness. Most gladly therefore will I rather glory in my infirmities, that the power of Christ may rest upon me."_ 2 Corinthians 12:9

**Question:** Do you realize now that some abilities are developed through courage and perseverance? Have you found some areas that God wants you to step out into that will not be easy, but you know He will be with you?

_____
_____
_____
_____

## STEP 4: Evaluating your Gifts and Abilities
### Week 16 — Dates: _____

**This Week's Goal:**
*Understand how the gifts of the Spirit operate.*

**This Week's Verse:**
*"Now there are diversities of gifts, but the same Spirit...
But the manifestation of the Spirit is given to every man
to profit withal...But all these worketh that one and the
selfsame Spirit, dividing to every man severally as he will."*
1 Corinthians 12:4, 7, 11

Now that you have looked at your natural abilities, trained talents and developed skills, it is time to consider the gifts of the Spirit. These gifts are unique, because we cannot claim any personal talent or ability when they operate through us. They are a distinct work of God that we could not come up with on our own.

The nine gifts of the spirit fall into three categories—knowledge, power and speech. This week, you will examine these gifts and understand how they are intended to operate in the Church.

| Prayer Requests | Answers to Prayer | Thanksgiving and Praise |
|---|---|---|
| | | |
| | | |
| | | |
| | | |
| | | |
| | | |
| | | |

**WEEK #16: Monday, _____**

*"Now there are diversities of gifts, but the same Spirit...*
*But the manifestation of the Spirit is given to every man to*
*profit withal...But all these worketh that one and the*
*selfsame Spirit, dividing to every man severally as he will."*
1 Corinthians 12:4, 7, 11

**Thought:** There are 9 gifts of the Spirit that God chooses to operate through human beings. He decides when, where and who will be involved.

**Question:** Are you familiar with the gifts of the Spirit? Have you seen all of them in operation at one time or another?

_____
_____
_____
_____
_____


**WEEK #16: Tuesday, _____**

*"Quench not the Spirit. Despise not prophesyings.*
*Prove all things; hold fast that which is good."*
1 Thessalonians 5:19-21

**Thought:** When God desires to use you in the gifts of the Spirit, it is important to yield to him, and not "quench" or put out the fire of the Spirit.

**Question:** Are you willing to let God use you in the gifts of the Spirit anywhere, anytime and any way He chooses to do so?

_____
_____
_____
_____
_____
_____

**WEEK #16: Wednesday, _____**

*"For to one is given by the Spirit the word of
wisdom; to another the word of knowledge by the
same Spirit...to another discerning of spirits..."*
1 Corinthians 12:8,10

**Thought:** Three gifts of the Spirit involve a supernatural knowledge — something beyond our human capability of knowing.

**Question:** Have you seen the gift of wisdom, knowledge or discerning of spirits in operation before? Has God ever used you in these gifts?

_____

_____

_____

_____

_____

**WEEK #16: Thursday, _____**

*"To another faith by the same Spirit; to
another the gifts of healing by the same Spirit;
To another the working of miracles..."*
1 Corinthians 12:9-10

**Thought:** Three gifts of the Spirit involve supernatural power — seeing things accomplished that a human is not capable of doing.

**Question:** Have you seen the gift of faith, healing or miracles in operation before? Has God ever used you in these gifts?

_____

_____

_____

_____

_____

## WEEK #16: Friday, _____

*"...to another prophecy...to another divers kinds of tongues; to another the interpretation of tongues:"*
1 Corinthians 12:10

**Thought:** Three of the gifts of the Spirit involve supernatural speech — saying something that a human could not have come up with on their own.

**Question:** Have you seen the gift of prophecy, tongues or interpretation of tongues in operation before? Has God ever used you in these gifts?

_____

_____

_____

_____

_____

_____


## WEEK #16: Saturday, _____

*"Even so ye, forasmuch as ye are zealous of spiritual gifts, seek that ye may excel to the edifying of the church."*
1 Corinthians 14:12

**Thought:** It is not wrong to desire the gifts of the Spirit, as long as our motive is right — wanting to help people and minister to them.

**Question:** Has God ever chosen to operate a gift of the Spirit through you? If not, would you like Him to?

_____

_____

_____

_____

_____

_____

*"Let all things be done decently and in order."*
1 Corinthians 14:40

**Thought:** God intends for the gifts of the Spirit to be used in an appropriate way, and under the direction of the spiritual authority in the church — the pastor.

**Question:** Have you ever seen the gifts of the Spirit used inappropriately? Are you ministered to when the gifts are used appropriately?

_____

_____

_____

_____

_____

# WEEK #16: REVIEW

**This Week's Goal:**
*Understand how the gifts of the Spirit operate.*

**This Week's Verse:**
*"Now there are diversities of gifts, but the same Spirit...
But the manifestation of the Spirit is given to every man
to profit withal...But all these worketh that one and the
selfsame Spirit, dividing to every man severally as he will."*
1 Corinthians 12:4,7,11

**Question:** Have you learned more about the gifts of the Spirit this week? Do you feel like you are ready and willing for God to use you in these areas, if He chooses to? Will you keep a good attitude and make sure God gets the glory?

_____

_____

_____

_____

_____

# ORDER MY STEPS
# Devotional Journal

## STEP 5:
## Becoming
## Aware of Needs

## STEP 5: Becoming Aware of Needs

It is time to take another inventory! When you finish, check back to your last evaluation. Are you making progress, especially in the area of developing your gifts and abilities?

This month, you are going to focus on becoming aware of needs; both your own needs and the needs of others. This is a vital part of learning how to be used of God to minister to others. It is too easy to fall into the rut of just living your own life, without being conscious of when others need help.

The Golden Rule says to "Do unto others as you would have them do unto you" (Luke 6:31 paraphrased). That is why becoming aware of your own needs first will help you to understand the needs of others.

| Area of your life to evaluate: | Weak, Good or Great |
|---|---|
| Relationship with God as your Father | |
| Emotional and physical condition | |
| Self-image and purpose in life | |
| Development of gifts and abilities | |
| Awareness of others' needs | |
| Reaching out to others | |
| Recognizing God's voice | |
| Obeying God's direction | |
| Self-discipline and spiritual habits | |
| Relationship with God as your friend | |

You are on a journey to closeness with God and ministry to others. Hang in there!

## STEP 5: Becoming Aware of Needs
## Week 17 — Dates: _____

### This Week's Goal:
*Learn how to recognize your own needs.*

### This Week's Verse:
*"And the very God of peace sanctify you wholly; and I pray God your whole spirit and soul and body be preserved blameless unto the coming of our Lord Jesus Christ."*
1 Thessalonians 5:23

God created each of us — body, soul and spirit. He knows exactly what we need in order to function properly. Life has the potential to get so busy that we overlook our own needs, and this can lead to burnout. God wants you to let your light shine, not to let it burn out!

It is not selfish to take time to make sure your own needs are met — it will cause your ministry to others to be more effective and long lasting. In order to love others as yourself, you have to be kind to yourself! God expects us to take care of the bodies we are given to live in.

| Prayer Requests | Answers to Prayer | Thanksgiving and Praise |
|---|---|---|
| | | |
| | | |
| | | |
| | | |
| | | |
| | | |
| | | |

**WEEK #17: Monday, _____**

*"And the very God of peace sanctify you wholly; and I*
*pray God your whole spirit and soul and body be preserved*
*blameless unto the coming of our Lord Jesus Christ."*
1 Thessalonians 5:23

**Thought:** God does not just care about your soul. He created you, and He cares about every aspect of your life, including your body and your spirit.

**Question:** Have you ever thought that God would not pay attention to your physical and emotional needs, only to your spiritual needs? Did you realize later you were wrong?

_____
_____
_____
_____
_____
_____


**WEEK #17: Tuesday, _____**

*"And he said unto them, Come ye yourselves apart into a*
*desert place, and rest a while: for there were many coming*
*and going, and they had no leisure so much as to eat."*
Mark 6:31

**Thought:** The disciples got so busy working for Jesus that they ignored their physical needs of rest and food. Jesus had to remind them about these needs.

**Question:** Have you ever gotten so busy working for God that you have neglected your own physical needs?

_____
_____
_____
_____
_____

**WEEK #17: Wednesday,** _____

*"Know ye not that ye are the temple of God,*
*and that the Spirit of God dwelleth in you?"*
1 Corinthians 3:16

**Thought:** We should respect and take care of our bodies in the same way we respect and take care of the church we worship in.

**Question:** Do you respect and take care of your body? Do you realize that since God lives inside you, you need to do this?

_____
_____
_____
_____
_____
_____

**WEEK #17: Thursday,** _____

*"But I keep under my body, and bring it into*
*subjection: lest that by any means, when I have*
*preached to others, I myself should be a castaway."*
1 Corinthians 9:27

**Thought:** Paul realized that although he had physical needs, the most important thing was that his soul be saved.

**Question:** Do you wrestle with physical desires that could have a negative impact on your soul? Have you developed self-discipline in these areas, for your soul's sake?

_____
_____
_____
_____
_____
_____

*"For whosoever will save his life shall lose it: and whosoever will lose his life for my sake shall find it. For what is a man profited, if he shall gain the whole world, and lose his own soul? or what shall a man give in exchange for his soul?"*
Matthew 16:25-26

**Thought:** Our ultimate need is for our souls to be saved. No other need is greater than this.

**Question:** If you ever had to choose between saving your life and saving your soul, do you believe God would give you the strength to die for Him?

_____

_____

_____

_____

_____

*"Therefore we were comforted in your comfort: yea, and exceedingly the more joyed we for the joy of Titus, because his spirit was refreshed by you all."*
2 Corinthians 7:13

**Thought:** Each of us has needs in our spirit — refreshing and encouragement. Being in a good frame of mind makes everything we do much easier.

**Question:** Are you aware of the needs of your spirit — things to do with your mind and emotions? Have you ever tried functioning with a discouraged spirit?

_____

_____

_____

_____

_____

*"And be renewed in the spirit of your mind;"*
Ephesians 4:23

**Thought:** God intends for us to keep coming back to Him to have the spirit of our mind renewed, so we can function in faith, confidence and encouragement!

**Question:** Do you go to God to be renewed when your spirit is downcast?

_____

_____

_____

_____

_____

## WEEK #17: REVIEW

### This Week's Goal:
*Learn how to recognize your own needs.*

### This Week's Verse:
*"And the very God of peace sanctify you wholly; and I pray God your whole spirit and soul and body be preserved blameless unto the coming of our Lord Jesus Christ."*
1 Thessalonians 5:23

**Question:** What have you learned this week about recognizing your own needs? Have you been denying your needs instead of allowing God to meet them? How are things going to change from now on?

_____

_____

_____

_____

_____

_____

## STEP 5: Becoming Aware of Needs
### Week 18 — Dates: _____

### This Week's Goal:
*Pay attention to the physical needs of those around you.*

### This Week's Verse:
*"...Lord, when saw we thee an hungred, and fed thee?
or thirsty, and gave thee drink?...a stranger, and took thee in?
or naked, and clothed thee?...sick, or in prison, and came
unto thee?..Inasmuch as ye have done it unto one of the
least of these my brethren, ye have done it unto me."*
Matthew 25:37-40

Now that you are able to recognize your own needs, it is time to consider the needs of those around you. The most obvious needs are physical needs. You may discover physical needs in your family, your Christian brothers and sisters, your neighbours, your co-workers, your friends, or out in your community. If you are able to meet someone's physical need, go ahead and do it! Jesus counts it as being done to Him. Let's learn to see Jesus in the eyes of those in need!

| Prayer Requests | Answers to Prayer | Thanksgiving and Praise |
|---|---|---|
|  |  |  |
|  |  |  |
|  |  |  |
|  |  |  |
|  |  |  |
|  |  |  |
|  |  |  |

## WEEK #18: Monday, _____

*"...Lord, when saw we thee an hungred, and fed thee?
or thirsty, and gave thee drink?...a stranger, and took thee in?
or naked, and clothed thee?...sick, or in prison, and came
unto thee?..Inasmuch as ye have done it unto one of the
least of these my brethren, ye have done it unto me."*
Matthew 25:37-40

**Thought:** When you meet someone's physical need, it is as if you had done it directly for Jesus.

**Question:** When you feed, clothe, house or visit someone in need, are you aware that you are doing it for Jesus? Does this help you do it with a proper motive?

_____

_____

_____

_____


## WEEK #18: Tuesday, _____

*"...The ground of a certain rich man brought forth
plentifully...And he said...I will pull down my barns, and
build greater...And I will say to my soul...take thine ease,
eat, drink, and be merry. But God said unto him, Thou
fool, this night thy soul shall be required of thee..."*
Luke 12:16-20

**Thought:** When God blesses you, He does not intend for you to hoard it to yourself. He blesses you so that you can help others.

**Question:** When you receive a financial blessing, are you pleased because you can buy more things for yourself, or because you can help others with it?

_____

_____

_____

_____

**WEEK #18: Wednesday, _____**

*"And in those days, when the number of the disciples was multiplied, there arose a murmuring of the Grecians against the Hebrews, because their widows were neglected in the daily ministration."*
Acts 6:1

**Thought:** When it comes to our attention that a church member is in need, and we are able to help them, we need to do more than just pray for them!

**Question:** When you are made aware of a need in the church, do you think that someone else will take care of it, or do you give what you have available?

_____
_____
_____
_____
_____


**WEEK #18: Thursday, _____**

*"Pure religion and undefiled before God and the Father is this, To visit the fatherless and widows in their affliction, and to keep himself unspotted from the world."*
James 1:27

**Thought:** Those who are left without someone to support them especially need our help. God's idea of a true Christian is someone who notices and helps them.

**Question:** Do you know anyone who is in need because they have been left without a supporter, or breadwinner? What have you done to help them?

_____
_____
_____
_____
_____

## WEEK #18: Friday, _____

*"And all that believed were together, and had all things common; And sold their possessions and goods, and parted them to all men, as every man had need."*
Acts 2:44-45

**Thought:** The early apostolic Church had a beautiful, unselfish attitude. They considered that what God gave them was to be shared with those in need.

**Question:** Do you have this kind of attitude toward your possessions? If God asked you to give what you have to someone else, would you do it?

_____
_____
_____
_____
_____
_____
_____

## WEEK #18: Saturday, _____

*"Give to him that asketh thee, and from him that would borrow of thee turn not thou away."*
Matthew 5:42

**Thought:** Some people only want to help those who do not ask for help. The Bible says to help those who ask too!

**Question:** What kind of attitude do you have when someone asks you for something that they need?

_____
_____
_____
_____
_____
_____

*"And whosoever shall give to drink unto one of these little
ones a cup of cold water only in the name of a disciple,
verily I say unto you, he shall in no wise lose his reward."*
Matthew 10:42

**Thought:** God notices every effort you make to help someone,
no matter how small it is, and will reward you.

**Question:** Do you keep a good attitude when you help
someone and they are not thankful? Is God's reward enough
for you?

_____

_____

_____

_____

## WEEK #18: REVIEW

### This Week's Goal:
*Pay attention to the physical needs of those around you.*

### This Week's Verse:
*"...Lord, when saw we thee an hungred, and fed thee? or
thirsty, and gave thee drink?...a stranger, and took thee in? or
naked, and clothed thee?...sick, or in prison, and came unto
thee?..Inasmuch as ye have done it unto one of the least of
these my brethren, ye have done it unto me."*
Matthew 25:37-40

**Question:** Do you feel like this week has helped you become
more aware of the physical needs of those around you? Have
you discovered any attitudes toward helping others that may
need changing? Do you understand that when you help
others, it is as if you are helping God?

_____

_____

_____

_____

_____

## STEP 5: Becoming Aware of Needs
### Week 19 — Dates: _____

**This Week's Goal:**
*Be conscious of the emotional needs of those around you.*

**This Week's Verse:**
*"We then that are strong ought to bear the infirmities
of the weak, and not to please ourselves."*
Romans 15:1

As you learned last week, physical needs are the easiest to recognize. However, people tend to hide their emotional needs behind a mask of cheerfulness, success or unconcern. Hidden emotional needs do not disappear; instead they eat away at a person's spirit like a cancer.

As Christians, we need to ask God to help us to recognize when someone is hurting emotionally, so that we can minister to them. God can give you the wisdom and discernment to look below the surface of someone's life and see their emotional needs.

| Prayer Requests | Answers to Prayer | Thanksgiving and Praise |
|---|---|---|
|  |  |  |
|  |  |  |
|  |  |  |
|  |  |  |
|  |  |  |
|  |  |  |
|  |  |  |

## WEEK #19: Monday, _____

*"We then that are strong ought to bear the infirmities
of the weak, and not to please ourselves."*
Romans 15:1

**Thought:** God expects us as Christians to be unselfish with our time, and to minister to the needs of those who are hurting emotionally.

**Question:** When you know someone is hurting emotionally, do you feel a responsibility to try to help them?

_____
_____
_____
_____
_____
_____
_____

## WEEK #19: Tuesday, _____

*"Bear ye one another's burdens,
and so fulfil the law of Christ."*
Galatians 6:2

**Thought:** Jesus was our perfect example of bearing the burdens of others. When He saw a need, He ministered to it.

**Question:** Have you asked Jesus to make you more like Him in the area of helping others with the things that are burdening them emotionally?

_____
_____
_____
_____
_____
_____
_____

## WEEK #19: Wednesday, _____

*"For I perceive that thou art in the gall of bitterness, and in the bond of iniquity."*
Acts 8:23

**Thought:** Jesus gave Peter the ability to look beyond Simon's actions and see what his heart was really like.

**Question:** Do you take people at face value? Have you ever overlooked someone's real needs? Have you asked God to help you see below the surface?

_____

_____

_____

_____

_____

_____

_____


## WEEK #19: Thursday, _____

*"I have shewed you all things, how that so labouring ye ought to support the weak, and to remember the words of the Lord Jesus, how he said, It is more blessed to give than to receive."*
Acts 20:35

**Thought:** God blesses those who will help people who are feeling weak and discouraged.

**Question:** When you find out that someone needs strength and encouragement, what do you do?

_____

_____

_____

_____

_____

_____

_____

**WEEK #19: Friday, _____**

*"Now we exhort you, brethren, warn them that
are unruly, comfort the feebleminded, support
the weak, be patient toward all men."*
1 Thessalonians 5:14

**Thought:** People with emotional needs sometimes take a long time to recover. They need people who will patiently encourage them through the whole process.

**Question:** How is your patience level towards someone with an emotional need? Do you expect them to change overnight or do you give them time to heal?

_____

_____

_____

_____

_____

_____


**WEEK #19: Saturday, _____**

*"Wherefore lift up the hands which hang down, and the feeble
knees; And make straight paths for your feet, lest that which is
lame be turned out of the way; but let it rather be healed."*
Hebrews 12:12-13

**Thought:** God intends healing for those who are about to give up. His Church needs to be there to help so these people do not lose their way.

**Question:** Do you know of anyone who might be at the "end of their rope"? What have you done to help them?

_____

_____

_____

_____

_____

_"Watch and pray, that ye enter not into temptation:_
_the spirit indeed is willing, but the flesh is weak."_
Matthew 26:41

**Thought:** If someone is struggling, it does not necessarily mean they do not want to do God's will. Pray for their spirit to be strengthened so they can do what is right.

**Question:** When someone is struggling emotionally, do you tend to criticize them or pray for them?

_____

_____

_____

_____

_____

_____

## WEEK #19: REVIEW

### This Week's Goal:
_Become aware of the emotional needs of those around you._

### This Week's Verse:
_"We then that are strong ought to bear the infirmities_
_of the weak, and not to please ourselves."_
Romans 15:1

**Question:** What have you learned about emotional needs this week? Have you asked God to help you see past people's masks? Are you willing to let God use you to minister to someone's emotional needs?

_____

_____

_____

_____

_____

_____

## STEP 5: Becoming Aware of Needs
### Week 20 — Dates: _____

**This Week's Goal:**
*Become aware of the spiritual needs of those around you.*

**This Week's Verse:**
*"For the Son of man is come to seek
and to save that which was lost."*
Luke 19:10

God cares about our physical and emotional needs, but His main concern is that our souls be saved. This was the whole purpose of His coming to earth, ministering for 3 ½ years, training disciples, and giving His life as a sacrifice for our sins. Eternal needs are always the most important.

It is easy in our busy lifestyle to forget that the people we meet each day who do not know Jesus may lose their souls unless someone witnesses to them and intercedes for them. We need to become more soul-conscious. Instead of seeing faces and bodies around us, we need to realize that each person has a soul with an eternal destination. We may play a part in the future of their souls.

| Prayer Requests | Answers to Prayer | Thanksgiving and Praise |
|---|---|---|
|  |  |  |
|  |  |  |
|  |  |  |
|  |  |  |
|  |  |  |
|  |  |  |
|  |  |  |

**WEEK #20: Monday, _____**

*"For the Son of man is come to seek
and to save that which was lost."*
Luke 19:10

**Thought:** The heartbeat of God is to find lost souls and show them how to be saved.

**Question:** Are you concerned about souls? Do you need to ask God to give you a greater burden for the lost?

_____
_____
_____
_____
_____


**WEEK #20: Tuesday, _____**

*"There was a man...named Nicodemus...The same
came to Jesus by night, and said unto him, Rabbi, we
know that thou art a teacher come from God: for no
man can do these miracles that thou doest, except God
be with him. Jesus answered and said unto him, Verily,
verily, I say unto thee, Except a man be born again,
he cannot see the kingdom of God."*
John 3:1-3

**Thought:** When Nicodemus came to Jesus, Jesus got right to the point and told him how his soul could be saved.

**Question:** When someone talks to you about religion or God or spiritual things, do you try to turn the conversation to the needs of their soul?

_____
_____
_____
_____
_____

## WEEK #20: Wednesday, _____

*"And Philip ran thither to him, and heard him read the prophet Esaias, and said, Understandest thou what thou readest?...Then Philip opened his mouth, and began at the same scripture, and preached unto him Jesus."*
Acts 8:30, 35

**Thought:** When God sent Philip to speak to the Ethiopian eunuch, Philip realized that although the eunuch was reading God's Word, he did not know what it meant.

**Question:** When someone indicates that they read the Bible, do you assume that they know how to be saved, or do you ask questions to find out and make sure they know what to do?

_____
_____
_____
_____
_____

## WEEK #20: Thursday, _____

*"But Paul cried with a loud voice, saying, Do thyself no harm: for we are all here. Then he called for a light, and sprang in, and came trembling, and fell down before Paul and Silas, And brought them out, and said, Sirs, what must I do to be saved?"*
Acts 16:28-30

**Thought:** Paul and Silas cared more about the spiritual need of their jailer than they cared about their own chance to escape from jail.

**Question:** What means more to you — your own comfort, or the salvation of a lost soul?

_____
_____
_____
_____
_____

*"And a certain Jew named Apollos...came to Ephesus...and being fervent in the spirit, he spake and taught diligently the things of the Lord, knowing only the baptism of John...whom when Aquila and Priscilla had heard, they took him unto them, and expounded unto him the way of God more perfectly."*
Acts 18:24-26

**Thought:** Aquila and Priscilla recognized the need of a preacher for more truth, and they lovingly showed it to him in a way he could understand and receive.

**Question:** What is your attitude toward people of other religious denominations? Do you criticize and condemn, or look for an opportunity to help each other grow spiritually?

_____
_____
_____
_____

*"Brethren, if a man be overtaken in a fault, ye which are spiritual, restore such an one in the spirit of meekness; considering thyself, lest thou also be tempted."*
Galatians 6:1

**Thought:** God intends for us to respond to the spiritual needs of our fellow Christians in a humble and caring way.

**Question:** How do you act when another Christian makes a mistake? Do you allow pride or gossip in your life, or do you humbly try to help them?

_____
_____
_____
_____

*"Not forsaking the assembling of ourselves together, as
the manner of some is; but exhorting one another: and
so much the more, as ye see the day approaching."*
Hebrews 10:25

**Thought:** Our fellow Christians have spiritual needs of encouragement and fellowship. We have a responsibility to each other in this area.

**Question:** Do you feel like you are fulfilling your responsibility to your fellow Christians in the area of encouragement and fellowship?

_____
_____
_____
_____
_____
_____

## WEEK #20: REVIEW

**This Week's Goal:**
*Be conscious of the spiritual needs of those around you.*

**This Week's Verse:**
*"For the Son of man is come to seek
and to save that which was lost."*
Luke 19:10

**Question:** What did you learn this week about the spiritual needs of those around you — both the saved and the lost? Do you feel like you are becoming more soul-conscious?

_____
_____
_____
_____
_____
_____

# ORDER MY STEPS
## Devotional Journal

## STEP 6:
Reaching
Out to Others

## STEP 6: Reaching Out to Others

It is inventory time again. Check back to last month's evaluation. How are you coming along? Has there been an improvement in your awareness of others' needs?

This month, you are going to concentrate on reaching out to others. It isn't enough to be aware of the needs around you; you need to make a conscious effort to minister to those needs as God directs and enables you.

The first way you can reach out to others is by praying for them. Secondly, you can help those in your circle of influence — at home, school or work, and in your neighbourhood and community. Thirdly, you can get involved in church programs and ministries that help others. Fourthly, you can ask the Lord to lead you to someone to whom you can teach God's Word. Each of us are called to spread the Gospel!

| Area of your life to evaluate: | Weak, Good or Great |
|---|---|
| Relationship with God as your Father | |
| Emotional and physical condition | |
| Self-image and purpose in life | |
| Development of gifts and abilities | |
| Awareness of others' needs | |
| Reaching out to others | |
| Recognizing God's voice | |
| Obeying God's direction | |
| Self-discipline and spiritual habits | |
| Relationship with God as your friend | |

You are learning to let God use you; keep going and let Him lead you every day!

## STEP 6: Reaching Out to Others
### Week 21 — Dates: _____

### This Week's Goal:
*Understand your responsibility to pray for others.*

### This Week's Verse:
*"Moreover as for me, God forbid that I should sin
against the LORD in ceasing to pray for you:
but I will teach you the good and the right way:"*
1 Samuel 12:23

As Christians, each of us has a responsibility to pray for others. It's easy to remember to pray for our loved ones, but we need to reach out farther than that. Have you made yourself available to pray for others? Have you learned to recognize the call to prayer and obey it, even when it comes at an inconvenient time?

There may be seasons in your life when you have more time to pray than before. When life is one big whirlwind with small children, try to get up before they do, to pray. You can also pray in snatches as you go about your day. Use your "empty nest" season to develop a stronger prayer ministry. When you are confined because of sickness, let God pray through you for others. There is no excuse not to pray!

| Prayer Requests | Answers to Prayer | Thanksgiving and Praise |
|---|---|---|
| | | |
| | | |
| | | |
| | | |
| | | |
| | | |
| | | |

## WEEK #21: Monday, _____

*"Moreover as for me, God forbid that I should sin*
*against the LORD in ceasing to pray for you:*
*but I will teach you the good and the right way:"*
1 Samuel 12:23

**Thought:** God has placed people in your life who He expects you to pray for. Anyone with whom you have regular contact should be on your prayer list.

**Question:** Do you pray regularly for your family and friends? How about your neighbours and co-workers?

_____

_____

_____

_____

_____

_____

_____

## WEEK #21: Tuesday, _____

*"And forgive us our debts, as we forgive our debtors."*
Matthew 6:11-12

**Thought:** The words "me" and "I" are not found in the prayer pattern Jesus gave us known as "The Lord's Prayer".

**Question:** How much of your prayer time is used for personal needs, and how much for the needs of others?

_____

_____

_____

_____

_____

_____

_____

## WEEK #21: Wednesday, _____

*"Confess your faults one to another, and pray one for another, that ye may be healed. The effectual fervent prayer of a righteous man availeth much."*
James 5:16

**Thought:** Allowing our prayer time be consumed with our own needs can lead to self-pity. That is why we are instructed to pray for each others' needs.

**Question:** Have you found that your faith increases when you make a conscious effort to pray for the needs of others rather than just your own?

_____

_____

_____

_____

_____

_____


## WEEK #21: Thursday, _____

*"I will both lay me down in peace, and sleep: for thou, LORD, only makest me dwell in safety."*
Psalm 4:8

**Thought:** There are many dangers facing us in today's society. We need God's protection on a daily basis.

**Question:** Do you cover your loved ones in prayer each day by pleading the blood of Jesus over them?

_____

_____

_____

_____

_____

_____

## WEEK #21: Friday, _____

*"We then that are strong ought to bear the infirmities*
*of the weak, and not to please ourselves."*
Romans 15:1

**Thought:** When someone is going through a crisis, their faith may be weak. It may be someone else's prayers that sustain them.

**Question:** Do you take time to pray for the people you know who are going through trials and tragedies, who may not have the strength to pray for themselves?

_____
_____
_____
_____
_____
_____

## WEEK #21: Saturday, _____

*"And all things are of God, who hath reconciled*
*us to himself by Jesus Christ, and hath given*
*to us the ministry of reconciliation;"*
2 Corinthians 5:18

**Thought:** God needs people who will pray for those who are distant from Him, so that reconciliation can happen.

**Question:** When you hear about someone who has failed God, do you gossip and criticize, or do you intercede in prayer for their reconciliation to God?

_____
_____
_____
_____
_____
_____

*"And I sought for a man among them, that should make
up the hedge, and stand in the gap before me for the land,
that I should not destroy it: but I found none."*
Ezekiel 22:30

**Thought:** God is looking for people who will take His hand
and the hand of the sinner and join them through prayer.

**Question:** Have you made yourself available as an intercessor,
or link, between God and sinners?

_____
_____
_____
_____
_____
_____

## WEEK #21: REVIEW

**This Week's Goal:**
*Understand your responsibility to pray for others.*

**This Week's Verse:**
*"Moreover as for me, God forbid that I should sin
against the LORD in ceasing to pray for you:
but I will teach you the good and the right way:"*
1 Samuel 12:23

**Question:** This week, have you become more aware of your
responsibility to pray for others? Are you going to do it?

_____
_____
_____
_____
_____
_____

## STEP 6: Reaching out to Others
## Week 22 — Dates: _____

### This Week's Goal:
*Become aware of how you can minister
to those in your circle of influence.*

### This Week's Verse:
*"That ye may be blameless and harmless, the sons of God,
without rebuke, in the midst of a crooked and perverse
nation, among whom ye shine as lights in the world;"*
Philippians 2:15

Do you realize that God has placed you where you are for a purpose? The people you work with or go to school with, who live in your neighbourhood and work in the stores you frequent, have souls! Do you take a personal interest in them or are they just faces to you?

Ask God to make you "soul-conscious", so that when you see a face, you think about that person's eternal destiny. If you do this, you will be quick to seize opportunities to speak to people about the Lord, and the difference He can make in their lives. You can be a light in your neighbourhood, your office, your school, and your community!

| Prayer Requests | Answers to Prayer | Thanksgiving and Praise |
|---|---|---|
|  |  |  |
|  |  |  |
|  |  |  |
|  |  |  |
|  |  |  |
|  |  |  |
|  |  |  |

*"That ye may be blameless and harmless, the sons of God, without rebuke, in the midst of a crooked and perverse nation, among whom ye shine as lights in the world;"*
Philippians 2:15

**Thought:** God has ordained that your life would stand out from the rest of the crowd, as His love shines through you.

**Question:** Do the people you come in contact with see something different about you? Do they feel God's love in the way you treat them?

_____

_____

_____

_____

_____

_____

*"And, ye fathers, provoke not your children to wrath: but bring them up in the nurture and admonition of the Lord."*
Ephesians 6:4

**Thought:** When reaching out to others, we cannot overlook those right in front of us. We have a huge responsibility to our children, to show them God's ways.

**Question:** Do your children feel God's love through you? Does it show in how you speak to them and discipline them?

_____

_____

_____

_____

_____

_____

*"Likewise, ye wives, be in subjection to your own husbands; that, if any obey not the word, they also may without the word be won by the conversation of the wives; While they behold your chaste conversation coupled with fear."*
1 Peter 3:1-2

**Thought:** The way we treat an unsaved spouse can be the cause of them coming to Christ.

**Question:** Do you minister God's love to your spouse, even when you do not feel like it?

_____

_____

_____

_____

_____

*"If a brother or sister be naked, and destitute of daily food, And one of you say unto them, Depart in peace, be ye warmed and filled; notwithstanding ye give them not those things which are needful to the body; what doth it profit?"*
James 2:15 16

**Thought:** There are some obvious needs that come to our attention, which require that we do more than pray for the need.

**Question:** When you see an obvious need such as food, clothing or finances, do you help in a practical way as well as praying for the person?

_____

_____

_____

_____

_____

_"But sanctify the Lord God in your hearts: and be ready
always to give an answer to every man that asketh you a
reason of the hope that is in you with meekness and fear:"_
1 Peter 3:15

**Thought:** God will place people in your life who will be
curious about your faith when they see your godly actions.

**Question:** Do you give an honest answer when someone
asks you about your godly lifestyle? Do you answer gently
and wisely?

_____

_____

_____

_____

_____


**WEEK #22: Saturday,** _____

_"Ye are our epistle written in our hearts, known and
read of all men: Forasmuch as ye are manifestly declared
to be the epistle of Christ ministered by us, written not
with ink, but with the Spirit of the living God; not in
tables of stone, but in fleshy tables of the heart."_
2 Corinthians 3:2-3

**Thought:** Some people may never open a Bible until they see
faith in action in someone's daily life.

**Question:** Are you conscious of the way you act and talk,
knowing it can affect someone else's spiritual destiny?

_____

_____

_____

_____

_____

*"But I say unto you, Love your enemies, bless them that curse you, do good to them that hate you, and pray for them which despitefully use you, and persecute you;"*
Matthew 5:44

**Thought:** Throughout our lives, we will undoubtedly come into contact with people who will mistreat us.

**Question:** Do you let God's love flow through you even to those who mistreat you? Do you respond properly to them?

_____
_____
_____
_____
_____

## WEEK #22: REVIEW

### This Week's Goal:
*Become aware of how you can minister to those in your circle of influence.*

### This Week's Verse:
*"That ye may be blameless and harmless, the sons of God, without rebuke, in the midst of a crooked and perverse nation, among whom ye shine as lights in the world;"*
Philippians 2:15

**Question:** This week, have you become more conscious of the people in your circle of influence and how you can minister to them?

_____
_____
_____
_____
_____
_____

## STEP 6: Reaching out to Others
### Week 23 — Dates: _____

**This Week's Goal:**
*Realize the value of being involved in a
ministry in your local church.*

**This Week's Verse:**
*"Now ye are the body of Christ, and members in
particular. And God hath set some in the church,
first apostles, secondarily prophets, thirdly teachers,
after that miracles, then gifts of healings, helps,
governments, diversities of tongues."*
1 Corinthians 12:27-28

When you were born, you became part of a family and a home. As you grew and matured, you were expected to take on new tasks and responsibilities. It takes everyone working together to have a peaceful and orderly home.

In the same way, when you were born again, you became part of a church family. As you grow spiritually, you will need to get more involved in the work of the church. Each member of a church must be active in order for the church to function properly. Each of us needs to find our place in the Body of Christ and be faithful to our responsibilities.

| Prayer Requests | Answers to Prayer | Thanksgiving and Praise |
|---|---|---|
|  |  |  |
|  |  |  |
|  |  |  |
|  |  |  |
|  |  |  |
|  |  |  |
|  |  |  |

### WEEK #23: Monday, _____

*"Now ye are the body of Christ, and members in*
*particular. And God hath set some in the church,*
*first apostles, secondarily prophets, thirdly teachers,*
*after that miracles, then gifts of healings, helps,*
*governments, diversities of tongues."*
1 Corinthians 12:27-28

**Thought:** There are many different ministries in the Church. All are necessary and the Church suffers if someone does not do their part.

**Question:** Have you ever thought that what you are doing in your church is unimportant or unnecessary?

_____

_____

_____

_____

_____

_____

### WEEK #23: Tuesday, _____

*"Not forsaking the assembling of ourselves together,*
*as the manner of some is; but exhorting one another:*
*and so much the more, as ye see the day approaching."*
Hebrews 10:25

**Thought:** Even your attendance to church services and activities makes a difference in the strength of the church.

**Question:** Are you faithful in attendance to your church? Do you let the pastor know when you are unable to attend?

_____

_____

_____

_____

_____

_____

## WEEK #23: Wednesday, _____

*"And they, continuing daily with one accord in the temple, and breaking bread from house to house, did eat their meat with gladness and singleness of heart, Praising God, and having favour with all the people. And the Lord added to the church daily such as should be saved."*
Acts 2:46-47

**Thought:** Unity is foundational to the health of a church. Amazing things can be accomplished when people work together for a common purpose.

**Question:** Are you in unity with your pastor and church family? Are you committed to the church's success?

_____

_____

_____

_____

_____

## WEEK #23: Thursday, _____

*"Now concerning the collection for the saints, as I have given order to the churches of Galatia, even so do ye. Upon the first day of the week let every one of you lay by him in store, as God hath prospered him, that there be no gatherings when I come."*
1 Corinthians 16:1-2

**Thought:** Just like a home or a business, a church needs operating funds. There are many expenses to cover.

**Question:** Are you faithful in giving tithes and offerings to support your pastor and the work of your church?

_____

_____

_____

_____

_____

## WEEK #23: Friday, _____

*"And when I come, whomsoever ye shall
approve by your letters, them will I send to
bring your liberality unto Jerusalem."*
1 Corinthians 16:3

**Thought:** Missions efforts also require operating funds, which local churches with a revival vision can provide.

**Question:** Do you support the missions program of your local church with your finances and prayers?

_____
_____
_____
_____
_____
_____

## WEEK #23: Saturday, _____

*"And a certain man lame from his mother's womb
was carried, whom they laid daily at the gate of the
temple which is called Beautiful, to ask alms of
them that entered into the temple;"*
Acts 3:2

**Thought:** There will be people in your church who need emotional and financial support. The church can minister to them in their time of need.

**Question:** Are you conscious of helping people in your church who carry heavy emotional or financial burdens?

_____
_____
_____
_____
_____
_____

_"Now there was at Joppa a certain disciple named Tabitha, which by interpretation is called Dorcas: this woman was full of good works and almsdeeds which she did....Then Peter arose and went with them. When he was come, they brought him into the upper chamber: and all the widows stood by him weeping, and shewing the coats and garments which Dorcas made, while she was with them."_
Acts 9:36, 39

**Thought:** The church needs your practical skills in order to have a complete ministry in the community.

**Question:** Are you using your practical skills to support the ministries of your church?

_____

_____

_____

_____

---

## WEEK #23: REVIEW

### This Week's Goal:
_Realize the value of being involved in a ministry in your local church._

### This Week's Verse:
_"Now ye are the body of Christ, and members in particular. And God hath set some in the church, first apostles, secondarily prophets, thirdly teachers, after that miracles, then gifts of healings, helps, governments, diversities of tongues."_
1 Corinthians 12:27-28

**Question:** This week, have you become more aware of your place in the church? Are you willing to do your part?

_____

_____

_____

_____

## STEP 6: Reaching out to Others
### Week 24 — Dates: _____

**This Week's Goal:**
*Discover the importance of teaching God's Word to others.*

**This Week's Verse:**
*"So shall my word be that goeth forth out
of my mouth: it shall not return unto me void, but
it shall accomplish that which I please, and it
shall prosper in the thing whereto I sent it."*
Isaiah 55:11

An important part of reaching out to others is taking every opportunity we can find to teach the Word of God. God's Word is anointed and inspired and alive; it has the power to change lives. The Bible is our road map for life. Without it we are walking blind.

No matter what problem or decision a person may be facing, they can find the answers they need in the Bible. It will not be our human wisdom or knowledge that will make the difference in their situation, but the Word of God can. There are many different opportunities to teach the Word; we need to watch for them and take advantage of them.

| Prayer Requests | Answers to Prayer | Thanksgiving and Praise |
|---|---|---|
| | | |
| | | |
| | | |
| | | |
| | | |
| | | |
| | | |

## WEEK #24: Monday, _____

*"So shall my word be that goeth forth out
of my mouth: it shall not return unto me void,
but it shall accomplish that which I please, and it
shall prosper in the thing whereto I sent it."*
Isaiah 55:11

**Thought:** God's Word will never be inadequate for any situation.

**Question:** How has God's Word helped you with a problem or decision you had to make?

_____
_____
_____
_____
_____
_____

## WEEK #24: Tuesday, _____

*"In whom the god of this world hath blinded the minds of
them which believe not, lest the light of the glorious gospel of
Christ, who is the image of God, should shine unto them."*
2 Corinthians 4:4

**Thought:** When someone allows God's Word to shine into their hearts, it will have a transforming effect.

**Question:** Can you think of someone who recently experienced a life transformation when they received God's Word and obeyed it?

_____
_____
_____
_____
_____
_____

*"But ye shall receive power, after that the Holy Ghost is come upon you: and ye shall be witnesses unto me both in Jerusalem, and in all Judaea, and in Samaria, and unto the uttermost part of the earth."*
Acts 1:8

**Thought:** When we are full of the Holy Ghost, we will have the power and confidence we need to witness to others.

**Question:** When do you have more boldness to witness; when you have not prayed or when you are full of the Spirit?

_____
_____
_____
_____
_____
_____

*"And that repentance and remission of sins should be preached in his name among all nations, beginning at Jerusalem. And ye are witnesses of these things."*
Luke 24:47-48

**Thought:** God's Word is to be taught everywhere, but you begin where you are!

**Question:** Is there someone you see regularly who you could ask about studying the Bible together?

_____
_____
_____
_____
_____
_____

## WEEK #24: Friday, _____

*"And your feet shod with the*
*preparation of the gospel of peace;"*
Ephesians 6:15

**Thought:** Part of our spiritual armour is being prepared to share the Gospel, in a peaceful attitude.

**Question:** Have you ever been guilty of proclaiming God's Word in an offensive or judgmental way?

_____
_____
_____
_____
_____
_____

## WEEK #24: Saturday, _____

*"That the generation to come might know them, even*
*the children which should be born; who should arise*
*and declare them to their children: That they might*
*set their hope in God, and not forget the works of God,*
*but keep his commandments:"*
Psalm 78:6-7

**Thought:** We have a responsibility to pass God's Word on to the next generation so that the Church never dies out.

**Question:** What are you doing to plant the Word of God in the next generation?

_____
_____
_____
_____
_____
_____

## WEEK #24: Sunday, _____

*"And these words, which I command thee this day, shall
be in thine heart: And thou shalt teach them diligently
unto thy children, and shalt talk of them when thou sittest
in thine house, and when thou walkest by the way, and
when thou liest down, and when thou risest up."*
Deuteronomy 6:6-7

**Thought:** God expects us to look for opportunities to teach His Word to our children.

**Question:** Do you talk to your children about God in the daily routines of life? Do you set aside time for family devotions?

_____

_____

_____

_____

## WEEK #24: REVIEW

### This Week's Goal:
*Discover the importance of teaching God's Word to others.*

### This Week's Verse:
*"So shall my word be that goeth forth out
of my mouth: it shall not return unto me void,
but it shall accomplish that which I please, and it
shall prosper in the thing whereto I sent it."*
Isaiah 55:11

**Question:** Have you learned how important it is to teach God's Word whenever you have opportunity? Are there any opportunities you are going to take advantage of this week?

_____

_____

_____

_____

_____

# ORDER MY STEPS
## Devotional Journal

# STEP 7:
## Recognizing
## God's Voice

# STEP 7: Recognizing God's Voice

In the Bible, God used many different methods to speak to His people. God is always speaking, but people are not always listening! He has many things to tell us if we will slow down and listen. We learn to recognize voices by hearing them over and over. When the phone rings and a long-time friend says "Hello", you immediately know who it is because you are familiar with the voice.

The more we listen to God, the easier we will recognize His voice. No, He doesn't often speak in an audible voice — if He did, we wouldn't need much faith! This month, we will explore some of the ways that God does speak to us, and learn how to distinguish His voice from other voices. Four of the main ways God speaks to us are through personal Bible study, through preaching and teaching, through other people, and directly to our hearts.

| Area of your life to evaluate: | Weak, Good or Great |
|---|---|
| Relationship with God as your Father | |
| Emotional and physical condition | |
| Self-image and purpose in life | |
| Development of gifts and abilities | |
| Awareness of others' needs | |
| Reaching out to others | |
| Recognizing God's voice | |
| Obeying God's direction | |
| Self-discipline and spiritual habits | |
| Relationship with God as your friend | |

Look at the progress you are making! Isn't it exciting to grow spiritually?

## STEP 7: Recognizing God's Voice
### Week 25 — Dates: _____

**This Week's Goal:**
*Learn to recognize how God speaks
to you through the Bible.*

**This Week's Verse:**
*"For the word of God is quick, and powerful, and sharper
than any twoedged sword, piercing even to the dividing
asunder of soul and spirit, and of the joints and marrow, and
is a discerner of the thoughts and intents of the heart."*
Hebrews 4:12

We have been given a treasure — the Word of God, or the "Bible" as we call it. God's people in countries where the Bible is banned have a deep and intense appreciation for it. We should never take God's Word for granted or allow it to collect dust in our home. We need to read and apply it to our lives daily.

The Bible has lasted for centuries; no one has been able to destroy it. It remains a best-seller in spite of the millions of books that have been written by human authors. Since the Bible was written under God's anointing, it still has the power to speak to our lives today. The Word is alive!

| Prayer Requests | Answers to Prayer | Thanksgiving and Praise |
|---|---|---|
| | | |
| | | |
| | | |
| | | |
| | | |
| | | |
| | | |

## WEEK #25: Monday, _____

*"For the word of God is quick, and powerful, and sharper than any twoedged sword, piercing even to the dividing asunder of soul and spirit, and of the joints and marrow, and is a discerner of the thoughts and intents of the heart."*
Hebrews 4:12

**Thought:** The Word of God can quickly identify a wrong motive or desire in our hearts.

**Question:** Can you think of a time when you were reading your Bible and God convicted you of a wrong motive?

_____
_____
_____
_____
_____
_____

## WEEK #25: Tuesday, _____

*"Thou hast commanded us to keep thy precepts diligently. O that my ways were directed to keep thy statutes! Then shall I not be ashamed, when I have respect unto all thy commandments."*
Psalm 119:4-6

**Thought:** If we do not seek counsel from God's Word, we may make bad decisions that will embarrass us later.

**Question:** Have you had God speak to you through His Word about a decision you had to make?

_____
_____
_____
_____
_____
_____

## WEEK #25: Wednesday, _____

*"Blessed is the man that walketh not in the counsel of the
ungodly, nor standeth in the way of sinners, nor sitteth in the
seat of the scornful. But his delight is in the law of the LORD;
and in his law doth he meditate day and night."*
Psalm 1:1-2

**Thought:** God wants to bless our lives, but He can only do
this if we study the Word and apply it to our lives.

**Question:** Do you study your Bible daily and ask God to
bring verses to your attention that you need to act on?

_____

_____

_____

_____

_____

## WEEK #25: Thursday, _____

*"Thy words were found, and I did eat them; and thy word
was unto me the joy and rejoicing of mine heart: for I
am called by thy name, O LORD God of hosts."*
Jeremiah 15:16

**Thought:** Just as we would run to the mailbox to get a letter
from a friend, we should desire to hear God's voice through
His Word.

**Question:** Do you love to read your Bible? If not, have you
asked God to give you a love for His Word?

_____

_____

_____

_____

_____

## WEEK #25: Friday, _____

*"Thy word is a lamp unto my feet, and a light unto my path."*
Psalm 119:105

**Thought:** Life can be confusing and uncertain if we rely on our own knowledge. God's Word brings clarity and understanding to every situation.

**Question:** Do you allow God to speak to you through His Word and give you direction when you are confused?

_____

_____

_____

_____

_____

_____


## WEEK #25: Saturday, _____

*"With my whole heart have I sought thee: O let me not wander from thy commandments. Thy word have I hid in mine heart, that I might not sin against thee."*
Psalm 119:10-11

**Thought:** If we regularly study the Bible, the principles that become ingrained in our hearts and minds will keep us from sinning.

**Question:** Have you ever started to do something and had a scripture come to your mind, to convict you that what you were about to do was not pleasing to God?

_____

_____

_____

_____

_____

_____

## WEEK #25: Sunday, _____

*"Order my steps in thy word: and let not
any iniquity have dominion over me."*
Psalm 119:133

**Thought:** If we study God's Word, it will point us in the direction He wants us to go.

**Question:** Are you allowing God's Word to direct your life — in your daily routines and in your big decisions?

_____

_____

_____

_____

_____

## WEEK #25: REVIEW

### This Week's Goal:
*Learn to recognize how God speaks
to you through the Bible.*

### This Week's Verse:
*"For the word of God is quick, and powerful, and sharper
than any twoedged sword, piercing even to the dividing
asunder of soul and spirit, and of the joints and marrow,
and is a discerner of the thoughts and intents of the heart."*
Hebrews 4:12

**Question:** Are you more aware now of how God can speak to you through His Word? As you read your Bible, take note of when a scripture "jumps out" at you, and let God speak to you about your life through it.

_____

_____

_____

_____

_____

## STEP 7: Recognizing God's Voice
## Week 26 — Dates: _____

### This Week's Goal:
*Understand how God speaks to you*
*through preaching and teaching.*

### This Week's Verse:
*"For after that in the wisdom of God the world by*
*wisdom knew not God, it pleased God by the*
*foolishness of preaching to save them that believe."*
1 Corinthians 1:21

Another way in which God speaks to us today is through preaching and teaching. This could be in a service, one-on-one, in a recorded sermon, or in a book; however God's Word is being proclaimed. It is important to have a steady dose of the Word of God.

There are many things in today's society that try to fill our minds. We are constantly bombarded by advertisements and the opinions of others. In order to safeguard our minds, we need to fill them with godly teaching. If our minds are already full of God's Word, there will be no room for false or foolish things.

| Prayer Requests | Answers to Prayer | Thanksgiving and Praise |
|---|---|---|
| | | |
| | | |
| | | |
| | | |
| | | |
| | | |
| | | |

_"For after that in the wisdom of God the world by
wisdom knew not God, it pleased God by the
foolishness of preaching to save them that believe."_
1 Corinthians 1:21

**Thought:** We may think we know a more effective way to save the world than through preaching, but God knows best.

**Question:** Do you get a steady dose of preaching and teaching by being faithful to your local church services?

_____

_____

_____

_____

_____


**WEEK #26: Tuesday,** _____

_"And Jonah began to enter into the city a day's journey,
and he cried, and said, Yet forty days, and Nineveh shall
be overthrown. So the people of Nineveh believed God,
and proclaimed a fast, and put on sackcloth, from the
greatest of them even to the least of them."_
Jonah 3:4-5

**Thought:** Nineveh was full of wickedness, but it was brought to its knees by the preaching of God's Word.

**Question:** Have you seen sinners who came to repentance because they heard God's voice through a preacher?

_____

_____

_____

_____

_____

*"Now when they heard this, they were pricked in their heart, and said unto Peter and to the rest of the apostles, Men and brethren, what shall we do? Then Peter said unto them, Repent, and be baptized every one of you in the name of Jesus Christ for the remission of sins, and ye shall receive the gift of the Holy Ghost."*
Acts 2:37-38

**Thought:** Anointed preaching will cause a response in hungry hearts.

**Question:** Do you allow God to speak to you through preaching? Do you respond to what He is saying to you?

_____

_____

_____

_____

*"And cast him out of the city, and stoned him: and the witnesses laid down their clothes at a young man's feet, whose name was Saul. And they stoned Stephen, calling upon God, and saying, Lord Jesus, receive my spirit."*
Acts 7:58-59

**Thought:** Stephen's preaching had such an effect on Saul that when God spoke directly to Saul later on the road to Damascus, he was ready to listen.

**Question:** Have you seen people's hearts softened by preaching over time?

_____

_____

_____

_____

_____

## WEEK #26: Friday, _____

*"So they read in the book in the law of God distinctly, and gave the sense, and caused them to understand the reading."*
Nehemiah 8:8

**Thought:** We may not understand everything we read in the Bible on our own, but anointed preaching can clarify it to us.

**Question:** Have you heard a preacher speak about a verse and bring out a fresh meaning that you had never noticed?

_____

_____

_____

_____

_____

_____

_____

## WEEK #26: Saturday, _____

*"Whoso despiseth the word shall be destroyed: but he that feareth the commandment shall be rewarded."*
Proverbs 13:13

**Thought:** We need to make sure we keep our hearts open to learn from the Word of God.

**Question:** Regardless of how long you have been serving God, are you open to let God speak to you through preaching or teaching?

_____

_____

_____

_____

_____

_____

_____

_____

*"These were more noble than those in Thessalonica, in that they received the word with all readiness of mind, and searched the scriptures daily, whether those things were so."*
Acts 17:11

**Thought:** God expects us to discern between true and false preaching by checking things out in the Bible.

**Question:** Have you ever had someone try to tell you something that contradicted God's written Word?

_____
_____
_____
_____
_____
_____

## WEEK #26: REVIEW

**This Week's Goal:**
*Understand how God speaks to you through preaching and teaching.*

**This Week's Verse:**
*"For after that in the wisdom of God the world by wisdom knew not God, it pleased God by the foolishness of preaching to save them that believe."*
1 Corinthians 1:21

**Question:** Has your study this week helped you to see how God can speak to you through preaching and teaching?

_____
_____
_____
_____
_____
_____

## STEP 7: Recognizing God's Voice
### Week 27 — Dates: _____

### This Week's Goal:
*Discover how God can speak to you*
*through the words of another person.*

### This Week's Verse:
*"But the manifestation of the Spirit is given*
*to every man to profit withal. For to one is given*
*by the Spirit the word of wisdom; to another*
*the word of knowledge by the same Spirit;"*
1 Corinthians 12:7-8

Another way in which God speaks to us is through the words of someone else, in one-on-one conversation. Often God will give someone insight into another person's situation and anoint them to speak words of wisdom or knowledge to that person.

It might not always be something comfortable to hear, because sometimes we need encouragement and other times we need correction. We need to maintain a humble spirit and be attentive to what God is saying to us. Again, the measuring stick is the written Word of God, which will never pass away. We use it as a guide to discern the things that are said to us.

| Prayer Requests | Answers to Prayer | Thanksgiving and Praise |
|---|---|---|
|  |  |  |
|  |  |  |
|  |  |  |
|  |  |  |
|  |  |  |
|  |  |  |
|  |  |  |

## WEEK #27: Monday, _____

*"But the manifestation of the Spirit is given to
every man to profit withal. For to one is given
by the Spirit the word of wisdom; to another
the word of knowledge by the same Spirit;"*
1 Corinthians 12:7-8

**Thought:** Sometimes God will speak to you through another person by giving them knowledge of your situation or wisdom about how you should proceed.

**Question:** Have you ever had someone speak wisdom into a situation in your life when you were totally confused?

_____

_____

_____

_____

_____

## WEEK #27: Tuesday, _____

*"The woman then left her waterpot, and went her way into
the city, and saith to the men, Come, see a man, which told
me all things that ever I did: is not this the Christ?"*
John 4:28-29

**Thought:** Jesus got the attention of the woman at the well by revealing His supernatural knowledge of her life.

**Question:** Have you ever had someone find out from God something about your life that they had no other way of knowing?

_____

_____

_____

_____

_____

## WEEK #27: Wednesday, _____

*"For I perceive that thou art in the gall of bitterness, and in the bond of iniquity. Then answered Simon, and said, Pray ye to the Lord for me, that none of these things which ye have spoken come upon me."*
Acts 8:23-24

**Thought:** When Simon asked for power to lay hands on people to receive the Holy Ghost, God gave Peter discernment into his real motives.

**Question:** Have you had someone allow God to use them to speak words of correction to you when you were off course?

_____
_____
_____
_____
_____


## WEEK #27: Thursday, _____

*"And as we tarried there many days, there came down from Judaea a certain prophet, named Agabus. And when he was come unto us, he took Paul's girdle, and bound his own hands and feet, and said, Thus saith the Holy Ghost, So shall the Jews at Jerusalem bind the man that owneth this girdle, and shall deliver him into the hands of the Gentiles."*
Acts 21:10-11

**Thought:** God may use someone else's words to prepare you for a trial you will go through.

**Question:** Have you had this happen in your life?

_____
_____
_____
_____
_____

*"Preach the word; be instant in season, out of season;
reprove, rebuke, exhort with all longsuffering and doctrine."*
2 Timothy 4:2

**Thought:** One of the things God expects your pastor to do is to patiently correct you when you are going the wrong way.

**Question:** Do you allow your pastor to speak to you about things he or she sees in your life that are a concern?

_____
_____
_____
_____
_____
_____
_____

*"Take heed, brethren, lest there be in any of you an evil heart
of unbelief, in departing from the living God. But exhort
one another daily, while it is called To day; lest any of
you be hardened through the deceitfulness of sin."*
Hebrews 3:12-13

**Thought:** God wants us to allow Him to speak words of encouragement and exhortation through us to each other.

**Question:** Do you listen to what other members of your church say to you, to encourage you in living for God?

_____
_____
_____
_____
_____
_____
_____

*"O LORD, I know that the way of man is not in himself:*
*it is not in man that walketh to direct his steps."*
Jeremiah 10:23

**Thought:** None of us can get spiritual enough to no longer
need constant direction from God in our lives.

**Question:** What is your attitude toward allowing God to
speak to you about your spiritual development?

_____

_____

_____

_____

_____

_____

## WEEK 27: REVIEW

### This Week's Goal:
*Discover how God can speak to*
*you through the words of another person.*

### This Week's Verse:
*"But the manifestation of the Spirit is given to*
*every man to profit withal. For to one is given by*
*the Spirit the word of wisdom; to another the*
*word of knowledge by the same Spirit;"*
1 Corinthians 12:7-8

**Question:** Through what you have learned this week about
God speaking to you through the words of others, has your
attitude changed to become more receptive to this?

_____

_____

_____

_____

_____

## STEP 7: Recognizing God's Voice
**Week 28 — Dates:** _____

### This Week's Goal:
*Understand how to hear God
speaking to your heart directly.*

### This Week's Verse:
*"Lead me in thy truth, and teach me: for thou art the
God of my salvation; on thee do I wait all the day."*
Psalm 25:5

God wants to talk to you! There are many things He wants to tell you, and if you are ready to listen, it will make your life a lot smoother, and you will grow spiritually. However, He waits for an invitation to come in. Just as a neighbour would knock on your door rather than barging in, God patiently does the same, and waits for a response.

If there is too much noise inside, or too many distractions in your mind, you may not hear God's knock. That's why it is so important to start your day in His presence, focusing completely on Him, and to take that listening attitude with you throughout the day. God sometimes shouts, but He usually whispers, so listen closely!

| Prayer Requests | Answers to Prayer | Thanksgiving and Praise |
|---|---|---|
|  |  |  |
|  |  |  |
|  |  |  |
|  |  |  |
|  |  |  |
|  |  |  |
|  |  |  |

## WEEK #28: Monday, _____

*"Lead me in thy truth, and teach me: for thou art the*
*God of my salvation; on thee do I wait all the day."*
Psalm 25:5

**Thought:** God wants to speak to you every day; He just waits for you to open the door and let Him in.

**Question:** Are you conscious of inviting God to speak to you every day, or is your day jammed full of other activities?

_____
_____
_____
_____
_____
_____
_____
_____

## WEEK #28: Tuesday, _____

*"And after the earthquake a fire; but the LORD was*
*not in the fire: and after the fire a still small voice."*
1 Kings 19:12

**Thought:** Elijah searched the wind, earthquake and fire for God's words, but found Him speaking in a still, small voice.

**Question:** Do you listen when God speaks to you quietly or do you think you He needs to be loud and dramatic?

_____
_____
_____
_____
_____
_____
_____
_____

_"And ere the lamp of God went out in the
temple of the LORD, where the ark of God was,
and Samuel was laid down to sleep; That the LORD
called Samuel: and he answered, Here am I."_
1 Samuel 3:3-4

**Thought:** Sometimes God waits till we are ready to sleep to speak to us, when all the other distractions have quieted.

**Question:** Do you listen for God's voice when you are preparing for sleep, or are you busy planning tomorrow?

_____
_____
_____
_____

**WEEK #28: Thursday,** _____

_"And a vision appeared to Paul in the night; There stood
a man of Macedonia, and prayed him, saying, Come over
into Macedonia, and help us. And after he had seen
the vision, immediately we endeavoured to go into
Macedonia, assuredly gathering that the Lord had
called us for to preach the gospel unto them."_
Acts 16:9-10

**Thought:** God can also speak to us through a dream which we remember clearly the next morning, since we do not usually remember most of our dreams.

**Question:** Have you ever had God tell you something through a dream?

_____
_____
_____
_____
_____

## WEEK #28: Friday, _____

*"While Peter thought on the vision, the Spirit
said unto him, Behold, three men seek thee. Arise
therefore, and get thee down, and go with them,
doubting nothing: for I have sent them."*
Acts 10:19-20

**Thought:** God got Peter's attention through a vision, and because of that the Gentiles got to experience salvation!

**Question:** Has God ever spoken to you through a vision (a dream while you are awake)?

_____

_____

_____

_____

_____

_____


## WEEK #28: Saturday, _____

*"And the word of the LORD came unto Jonah the second
time, saying, Arise, go unto Nineveh, that great city,
and preach unto it the preaching that I bid thee."*
Jonah 3:1-2

**Thought:** Just like Jonah, if we do not listen the first time, God will usually try to speak to us again.

**Question:** When you feel like you need to do something, and the thought just will not go away, do you pay attention? It could be God speaking to you.

_____

_____

_____

_____

_____

_____

*"For every one that useth milk is unskilful in the word of righteousness: for he is a babe. But strong meat belongeth to them that are of full age, even those who by reason of use have their senses exercised to discern both good and evil."*
Hebrews 5:13-14

**Thought:** We do not learn to recognize God's voice overnight. It takes practice and spiritual maturity.

**Question:** Do you feel like you can recognize God's voice easier now than when you first became a Christian?

_____
_____
_____
_____
_____
_____

## WEEK #28: REVIEW

**This Week's Goal:**
*Understand how to hear God
speaking to your heart directly.*

**This Week's Verse:**
*"Lead me in thy truth, and teach me: for thou art the
God of my salvation; on thee do I wait all the day."*
Psalm 25:5

**Question:** Do you recognize now the many ways God has tried to speak to you? Will you be more conscious of them?

_____
_____
_____
_____
_____
_____

# ORDER MY STEPS
## Devotional Journal

## STEP 8:
## Obeying
## God's Direction

# STEP 8: Obeying God's Direction

Over the past four weeks, you have been learning how to recognize God's voice. Now it is time to focus on obeying God's direction: doing what He has spoken to you to do. Our spiritual growth hinges on whether or not we will obey God and allow Him to order our steps.

The first way in which we obey God is to obey His Word and conform our lives to His principles. Secondly, it is very important that we submit to the authorities He has placed over us. The third thing we need to learn is to be led of His Spirit in our daily lives; in big and small things.

Finally, we need to make sure that we have a proper attitude in obeying God. If we will keep our ears open and always be obedient to the voice of God, we will develop an even closer relationship with Him than we have ever experienced.

| Area of your life to evaluate: | Weak, Good or Great |
| --- | --- |
| Relationship with God as your Father | |
| Emotional and physical condition | |
| Self-image and purpose in life | |
| Development of gifts and abilities | |
| Awareness of others' needs | |
| Reaching out to others | |
| Recognizing God's voice | |
| Obeying God's direction | |
| Self-discipline and spiritual habits | |
| Relationship with God as your friend | |

You have come a long way! God is pleased that you are drawing closer to Him.

## STEP 8: Obeying God's Direction
### Week 29 — Dates: _____

### This Week's Goal:
*Focus on obeying God as He shows you things in His Word.*

### This Week's Verse:
*"Then said Jesus to those Jews which believed on him, If ye continue in my word, then are ye my disciples indeed; And ye shall know the truth, and the truth shall make you free."*
John 8:31-32

We know we need to obey God's Word, but the Bible is a big book! He is constantly showing us new things in His Word that He wants us to do. It is a growth process that will not be finished until we are taken to heaven.

God wants to keep refining and polishing us, so that we will become more and more like Him. We need to keep letting Him teach us principles and attitudes from His Word. The more we obey Him, the more we will grow. It is our obedience to His Word that truly makes us His disciples, and it's the truth of His Word that brings real freedom to our lives.

| Prayer Requests | Answers to Prayer | Thanksgiving and Praise |
|---|---|---|
|  |  |  |
|  |  |  |
|  |  |  |
|  |  |  |
|  |  |  |
|  |  |  |
|  |  |  |

## WEEK #29: Monday, _____

*"Then said Jesus to those Jews which believed on him, If ye continue in my word, then are ye my disciples indeed; And ye shall know the truth, and the truth shall make you free."*
John 8:31-32

**Thought:** You will never exhaust all that there is to learn in God's Word. He wants you to continue learning and obeying.

**Question:** What have you learned recently from God's Word that He expected you to do? Did you obey?

_____
_____
_____
_____
_____
_____
_____

## WEEK #29: Tuesday, _____

*"But whoso looketh into the perfect law of liberty, and continueth therein, he being not a forgetful hearer, but a doer of the work, this man shall be blessed in his deed."*
James 1:25

**Thought:** It is not enough to read Gods Word and then go on our way unchanged. We need to act on what we read.

**Question:** When you see something in God's Word that indicates you need to change, do you do something about it?

_____
_____
_____
_____
_____
_____
_____

## WEEK #29: Wednesday, _____

*"Jesus said unto him, Thou shalt love the Lord thy God with all thy heart, and with all thy soul, and with all thy mind. This is the first and great commandment. And the second is like unto it, Thou shalt love thy neighbour as thyself. On these two commandments hang all the law and the prophets."*
Matthew 22:37-40

**Thought:** The two most basic commandments God expects us to obey are: loving God and loving people.

**Question:** Have you developed a deep love for God? Have you let Him develop in you a deep love for people?

_____
_____
_____
_____
_____
_____

## WEEK #29: Thursday, _____

*"Thou shalt have no other gods before me. Thou shalt not make unto thee any graven image, or any likeness of any thing that is in heaven above, or that is in the earth beneath, or that is in the water under the earth:"*
Exodus 20:3-4

**Thought:** Exodus 20:3-17 contains the Ten Commandments, the basic laws for living God's way.

**Question:** Do you govern your life by these ten laws that God gave, regardless of what our legal system allows?

_____
_____
_____
_____
_____
_____

## WEEK #29: Friday, _____

*"Then Peter said unto them, Repent, and be baptized every one of you in the name of Jesus Christ for the remission of sins, and ye shall receive the gift of the Holy Ghost. For the promise is unto you, and to your children, and to all that are afar off, even as many as the Lord our God shall call."*
Acts 2:38-39

**Thought:** God used the apostle Peter to first preach the message of New Testament Salvation. Eternal life is available to those who will obey it.

**Question:** Have you completely obeyed the plan of salvation? Do you teach it to your children and others?

_____

_____

_____

_____

_____

## WEEK #29: Saturday, _____

*"But the fruit of the Spirit is love, joy, peace, longsuffering, gentleness, goodness, faith, Meekness, temperance: against such there is no law. And they that are Christ's have crucified the flesh with the affections and lusts."*
Galatians 5:22-24

**Thought:** God expects us to allow the character qualities called the "fruit of the Spirit" to grow in our lives. When things do not go our way, we have opportunities to develop these qualities.

**Question:** Is the fruit of the Spirit growing in your life?

_____

_____

_____

_____

_"And beside this, giving all diligence, add to
your faith virtue; and to virtue knowledge; And to
knowledge temperance; and to temperance patience;
and to patience godliness; And to godliness brotherly
kindness; and to brotherly kindness charity."_
2 Peter 1:5-7

**Thought:** God expects us to actively develop Christian virtues. We will never reach a point where we do not need to learn anything more spiritually.

**Question:** Are you actively seeking to develop these Christian virtues in your life?

_____

_____

_____

_____

## WEEK #29: REVIEW

### This Week's Goal:
_Focus on obeying God as He shows you things in His Word._

### This Week's Verse:
_"Then said Jesus to those Jews which believed on him, If ye
continue in my word, then are ye my disciples indeed; And ye
shall know the truth, and the truth shall make you free."_
John 8:31-32

**Question:** Have you learned this week how important it is to continually study God's Word, and to ask Him to bring things to your attention that you need to be doing?

_____

_____

_____

_____

_____

## STEP 8: Obeying God's Direction
**Week 30 — Dates:** _____

### This Week's Goal:
*Realize the importance of submission
to those God has placed over you.*

### This Week's Verse:
*"Obey them that have the rule over you, and submit
yourselves: for they watch for your souls, as they that
must give account, that they may do it with joy, and
not with grief: for that is unprofitable for you."*
Hebrews 13:17

The owner of a company expects his employees to follow the directions given to them by the supervisors he has chosen. Spiritually, an important aspect of obeying God's direction is submitting to the people He has placed over us. They have the heavy responsibility of answering to God for our souls.

A parent's love for a child causes a protective instinct to arise. The child doesn't always understand all the rules that are made for the sake of safety. As Christians, we may not understand everything that is asked of us by our leaders, but God will honour our obedience if we do it as unto Him.

| Prayer Requests | Answers to Prayer | Thanksgiving and Praise |
|---|---|---|
| | | |
| | | |
| | | |
| | | |
| | | |
| | | |
| | | |

## WEEK #30: Monday, _____

*"Obey them that have the rule over you, and submit yourselves: for they watch for your souls, as they that must give account, that they may do it with joy, and not with grief: for that is unprofitable for you."*
Hebrews 13:17

**Thought:** It is easy to criticize our leaders, but we need to stop and think about the responsibility that they carry.

**Question:** What is your attitude toward leaders in your life? Do you criticize and complain or do you submit and obey?

_____

_____

_____

_____

_____

_____

_____

## WEEK #30: Tuesday, _____

*"Children, obey your parents in the Lord: for this is right. Honour thy father and mother; (which is the first commandment with promise;)"*
Ephesians 6:1-2

**Thought:** God expects children to obey their parents; and later when they are living on their own, to honour them.

**Question:** Did you obey your parents as a child? Do you honour your parents now that you are an adult?

_____

_____

_____

_____

_____

## WEEK #30: Wednesday, _____

*"Wives, submit yourselves unto your own
husbands, as unto the Lord. For the husband
is the head of the wife, even as Christ is the head
of the church: and he is the saviour of the body."*
Ephesians 5:22-23

**Thought:** If two people are trying to be in charge, chaos results. God placed the husband in charge of the family, reflecting God's relationship with the Church.

**Question:** Does your marriage reflect God's ordained order?

_____

_____

_____

_____

_____

## WEEK #30: Thursday, _____

*"And we beseech you, brethren, to know them which labour
among you, and are over you in the Lord, and admonish
you; And to esteem them very highly in love for their
work's sake. And be at peace among yourselves."*
1 Thessalonians 5:12-13

**Thought:** God expects us not only to obey our spiritual leaders, but to love and respect them. The result of this will be peace and unity in the Church.

**Question:** How do you treat your spiritual leaders? Do you obey, respect and love them?

_____

_____

_____

_____

_____

*"Servants, be obedient to them that are your masters according to the flesh, with fear and trembling, in singleness of your heart, as unto Christ; Not with eyeservice, as menpleasers; but as the servants of Christ, doing the will of God from the heart;"*
Ephesians 6:5-6

**Thought:** When we submit to our employers, we are doing it as unto God. Our submission should not just be outward, but God expects an inward submissive attitude.

**Question:** Do you submit to your employer, not just in your actions but in your attitude? Do you speak well of them?

_____

_____

_____

_____

_____

**WEEK #30: Saturday,** _____

*"Let every soul be subject unto the higher powers. For there is no power but of God: the powers that be are ordained of God. Whosoever therefore resisteth the power, resisteth the ordinance of God: and they that resist shall receive to themselves damnation."*
Romans 13:1-2

**Thought:** God expects us to obey governmental authorities, as long as they do not require us to disobey God, since He is the ultimate authority.

**Question:** Do you obey civil laws or try to get around them?

_____

_____

_____

_____

*"Submitting yourselves one to another in the fear of God."*
Ephesians 5:21

*"Wherefore, if meat make my brother to offend,*
*I will eat no flesh while the world standeth,*
*lest I make my brother to offend."*
1 Corinthians 8:13

**Thought:** Sometimes God will ask us to refrain from doing something we enjoy for the sake of not offending another Christian. Souls are more important than pleasure!

**Question:** Are you willing to obey God in this area?

_____
_____
_____
_____

## WEEK #30: REVIEW

### This Week's Goal:
*Realize the importance of submission*
*to those God has placed over you.*

### This Week's Verse:
*"Obey them that have the rule over you, and submit*
*yourselves: for they watch for your souls, as they that*
*must give account, that they may do it with joy, and*
*not with grief: for that is unprofitable for you."*
Hebrews 13:17

**Question:** This week, have you become more aware of the importance of submitting to the people God has placed over you? Do you realize it is part of your obedience to God?

_____
_____
_____
_____
_____

## STEP 8: Obeying God's Direction
### Week 31 — Dates: _____

**This Week's Goal:**
*Learn how to be led of the Spirit in your daily life.*

**This Week's Verse:**
*"For as many as are led by the Spirit
of God, they are the sons of God."*
Romans 8:14

God wants to lead you by His Spirit in your day-to-day life. It is important that you learn to let Him order your steps in both big and small decisions that you have to make. Without following His direction, you may miss many opportunities that He provides for ministering to others.

We make hundreds of small decisions each day, and many larger ones each week. Often when we have a decision to make, we look at the present facts and consider past experience. However, we are missing an important part of the equation: the future. God is the only one who knows what will happen next, and how our course will be affected by it. Only by seeking His guidance can we make proper decisions that will not cause us grief later.

| Prayer Requests | Answers to Prayer | Thanksgiving and Praise |
|---|---|---|
| | | |
| | | |
| | | |
| | | |
| | | |
| | | |
| | | |

## WEEK #31: Monday, _____

*"For as many as are led by the Spirit*
*of God, they are the sons of God."*
Romans 8:14

**Thought:** If we are truly God's children, we will allow His Spirit to lead us.

**Question:** Do you ask God every morning to lead your life that day?

_____
_____
_____
_____
_____
_____
_____
_____

## WEEK #31: Tuesday, _____

*"If we live in the Spirit, let us also walk in the Spirit."*
Galatians 5:25

**Thought:** If we are full of God's Spirit, it should show in how we live our daily lives.

**Question:** Are you conscious of seeking God's direction throughout the day as you go about your tasks?

_____
_____
_____
_____
_____
_____
_____
_____

## WEEK #31: Wednesday, _____

*"And being warned of God in a dream that
they should not return to Herod, they departed
into their own country another way."*
Matthew 2:12

**Thought:** God's Spirit will sometimes warn us of something
we need to avoid. If we ignore it, we will run into trouble.

**Question:** Have you ever had God warn you about something?
Did you pay attention? Were you glad that you did?

_____

_____

_____

_____

_____

_____

_____

## WEEK #31: Thursday, _____

*"Then was Jesus led up of the Spirit into the
wilderness to be tempted of the devil."*
Matthew 4:1

**Thought:** Sometimes God will lead you into a difficult
situation where your faith and trust will be tested.

**Question:** Do you submit with a humble, teachable attitude
when God leads you through a trial or test?

_____

_____

_____

_____

_____

_____

_____

## WEEK #31: Friday, _____

*"Then Peter said, Silver and gold have I none; but such as I have give I thee: In the name of Jesus Christ of Nazareth rise up and walk. And he took him by the right hand, and lifted him up: and immediately his feet and ankle bones received strength."*
Acts 3:6-7

**Thought:** God will often lead us to stop and minister to someone with whom we come in contact during the day.

**Question:** Do you keep your heart open for God to lead you to stop and minister to someone you see during the day?

_____
_____
_____
_____
_____

## WEEK #31: Saturday, _____

*"As they ministered to the Lord, and fasted, the Holy Ghost said, Separate me Barnabas and Saul for the work whereunto I have called them. And when they had fasted and prayed, and laid their hands on them, they sent them away."*
Acts 13:2-3

**Thought:** God's Spirit will speak to us about an area of ministry He wants us to move into, if we are listening.

**Question:** Do you fast and pray to keep an open heart so that God can lead you into the area of ministry He wants you to be involved in?

_____
_____
_____
_____
_____

*"Trust in the LORD with all thine heart; and
lean not unto thine own understanding. In all thy
ways acknowledge him, and he shall direct thy paths."*
Proverbs 3:5-6

**Thought:** Our human knowledge and the wisdom we have acquired is not enough. We need to daily seek God's direction.

**Question:** Do you rely on your own opinion when making decisions, or do you ask God to direct you?

_____
_____
_____
_____
_____
_____
_____

## WEEK #31: REVIEW

**This Week's Goal:**
*Learn how to be led of the Spirit in your daily life.*

**This Week's Verse:**
*"For as many as are led by the Spirit
of God, they are the sons of God."*
Romans 8:14

**Question:** Are you more conscious now of how God wants to lead you in your daily life? Have you decided to seek His direction in the big and small decisions?

_____
_____
_____
_____
_____
_____
_____

## STEP 8: Obeying God's Direction
### Week 32 — Dates: _____

### This Week's Goal:
*Decide to have a proper attitude in obeying God.*

### This Week's Verse:
*"...for the LORD seeth not as man seeth; for man looketh on the outward appearance, but the LORD looketh on the heart."*
1 Samuel 16:7

We have been learning how important it is to obey God, but we cannot overlook the importance of attitude. A child who obeys resentfully does not bring any joy to a parent. In the same way, we might obey God just to prevent negative consequences, but He sees through our actions to our heart. He knows if we have a proper motive and attitude.

Keeping a good attitude requires daily soul-searching and repentance. Our fleshly desires will constantly try to get between us and God. Keeping a good attitude is a full-time job, because life will test our attitude! When we offer our obedience to God with no false motives and out of love for Him, it is a beautiful offering that is pleasing to Him.

| Prayer Requests | Answers to Prayer | Thanksgiving and Praise |
|---|---|---|
|  |  |  |
|  |  |  |
|  |  |  |
|  |  |  |
|  |  |  |
|  |  |  |
|  |  |  |

## WEEK #32: Monday, _____

*"...for the LORD seeth not as man seeth; for man looketh on the outward appearance, but the LORD looketh on the heart."*
1 Samuel 16:7

**Thought:** We try to figure out other people's motives by what we see them do or say, but God sees what is inside people's hearts.

**Question:** Are you more conscious of how you appear to others or of the condition your heart is in?

_____

_____

_____

_____

_____

_____

_____

## WEEK #32: Tuesday, _____

*"Then Peter and the other apostles answered and said, We ought to obey God rather than men."*
Acts 5:29

**Thought:** Different people want different things from you, and it is impossible to please everyone. We need to focus our efforts on pleasing God by obeying Him.

**Question:** What means more to you, making people happy or making God happy?

_____

_____

_____

_____

_____

_____

_____

## WEEK #32: Wednesday, _____

*"And Samuel said, Hath the LORD as great delight
in burnt offerings and sacrifices, as in obeying the
voice of the LORD? Behold, to obey is better than
sacrifice, and to hearken than the fat of rams."*
1 Samuel 15:22

**Thought:** We can offer all kinds of things to God in an effort to get out of doing what He actually asked us to do, but our alternatives will not please Him.

**Question:** When God asks you to do something, do you obey completely, or do you try to find a more comfortable alternative?

_____

_____

_____

_____

_____

## WEEK #32: Thursday, _____

*"And Jesus said unto them, Come ye after me, and
I will make you to become fishers of men. And
straightway they forsook their nets, and followed him."*
Mark 1:17-18

**Thought:** When Jesus called the disciples to follow Him, they immediately stopped what they were doing and came.

**Question:** When God asks you to do something, do you obey quickly, or do you try to finish what you had planned first?

_____

_____

_____

_____

_____

## WEEK #32: Friday, _____

*"Whether therefore ye eat, or drink, or*
*whatsoever ye do, do all to the glory of God."*
1 Corinthians 10:31

**Thought:** People have many different motives for doing what they do. We need to make sure that our motive is to bring glory to God.

**Question:** What motivates you to do the things you do? Is it a desire for attention, a fear of consequences, or a desire to bring glory to God?

_____

_____

_____

_____

_____

_____

## WEEK #32: Saturday, _____

*"For God is not unrighteous to forget your work and labour*
*of love, which ye have shewed toward his name, in that*
*ye have ministered to the saints, and do minister."*
Hebrews 6:10

**Thought:** We can give many things to God: our time, our money, our talents, our loyalty......and these bring joy to God if we give them with a cheerful attitude.

**Question:** Do you give to God resentfully, feeling like you have to, or do you give out of a heart full of love and joy?

_____

_____

_____

_____

_____

_____

*"Seeing ye have purified your souls in obeying the truth through the Spirit unto unfeigned love of the brethren, see that ye love one another with a pure heart fervently:"*
1 Peter 1:22

**Thought:** God has called us to love one another, but He expects a real, selfless love, not a surface, pretend kind of love.

**Question:** Is your love for others just on the surface, or does it come from your heart?

_____

_____

_____

_____

_____

_____

_____

### WEEK #32: REVIEW

**This Week's Goal:**
*Decide to have a proper attitude in obeying God.*

**This Week's Verse:**
*"...for the LORD seeth not as man seeth; for man looketh on the outward appearance, but the LORD looketh on the heart."*
1 Samuel 16:7

**Question:** What have you learned this week about your attitude in obeying God? Did you find any attitudes in your heart that needed to change?

_____

_____

_____

_____

_____

_____

# ORDER MY STEPS
## Devotional Journal

## STEP 9:
## Developing
## Self-Discipline

# STEP 9: Developing Self-Discipline

We have been learning a lot of different things about how to get closer to God and progress spiritually. It is one thing to hear something and even to acknowledge that it is true; but it is another thing to put it into practice. The only way to see lasting change in your life is to develop self-discipline.

Godly self-discipline simply means that your "self" (body and mind) does not make the decisions in your life. God has decided what you should do, and because your heart and spirit are in tune with Him, you discipline your body and mind to do what God says — developing good spiritual habits. There are many areas of self-discipline that are beneficial; however this month we will focus on four critical areas: prayer & fasting, Bible study, stewardship, and holiness.

| Area of your life to evaluate: | Weak, Good or Great |
| --- | --- |
| Relationship with God as your Father | |
| Emotional and physical condition | |
| Self-image and purpose in life | |
| Development of gifts and abilities | |
| Awareness of others' needs | |
| Reaching out to others | |
| Recognizing God's voice | |
| Obeying God's direction | |
| Self-discipline and spiritual habits | |
| Relationship with God as your friend | |

Don't slow down now! Developing self-discipline will unlock many spiritual doors for you.

## STEP 9: Developing Self-Discipline
## Week 33 — Dates: _____

### This Week's Goal:
*Learn to discipline yourself to pray and fast.*

### This Week's Verse:
*"...If ye have faith as a grain of mustard seed, ye shall say unto this mountain, Remove hence to yonder place; and it shall remove; and nothing shall be impossible unto you. Howbeit this kind goeth not out but by prayer and fasting."*
Matthew 17:20-2

Prayer and fasting are two habits that are critical to your spiritual growth. Disciplining your mind to pray and your body to fast help to develop faith, because you become more in tune with God and more aware of what He wants to say and do through you. Just as you need water to survive physically, you need prayer to survive spiritually.

If you are by nature an introvert (not much of a talker), you may find it easier to study your Bible than to pray. However, both are extremely important. You will need to discipline yourself to set aside time to talk to God. The habit of fasting exercises your spiritual muscles, because the desire for food is one of the strongest human impulses; Esau sold his birthright for a bowl of soup when he was hungry!

| Prayer Requests | Answers to Prayer | Thanksgiving and Praise |
|---|---|---|
| | | |
| | | |
| | | |
| | | |
| | | |
| | | |
| | | |

## WEEK #33: Monday, _____

*"...If ye have faith as a grain of mustard seed, ye shall say
unto this mountain, Remove hence to yonder place; and
it shall remove; and nothing shall be impossible unto you.
Howbeit this kind goeth not out but by prayer and fasting."*
Matthew 17:20-21

**Thought:** Regular prayer and fasting will help to strengthen your faith in God. Faith starts as a seed and then grows.

**Question:** Is your faith in God weak or strong? Have you tried to develop it through regular prayer and fasting?

_____

_____

_____

_____

_____

_____

## WEEK #33: Tuesday, _____

*"Now Peter and John went up together into the temple
at the hour of prayer, being the ninth hour."*
Acts 3:1

**Thought:** The apostles had a regular time to pray each day. It was an appointment they planned their day around.

**Question:** Do you have an "hour of prayer" set aside in your schedule each day? When is your daily appointment with God?

_____

_____

_____

_____

_____

_____

**WEEK #33: Wednesday, _____**

*"Give us this day our daily bread."*
Matthew 6:11

**Thought:** God invites us to bring our needs before Him in prayer on a daily basis. We should not wait until we are starving to ask Him for our spiritual food.

**Question:** Do you eat only late at night, or in the morning so that you have energy for the day? Do you ask for your spiritual food at the beginning of the day?

_____
_____
_____
_____
_____

**WEEK #33: Thursday, _____**

*"And in the morning, rising up a great while before day, he went out, and departed into a solitary place, and there prayed."*
Mark 1:35

**Thought:** Jesus was God in flesh, but that flesh needed the discipline of prayer. Jesus chose a time and place when He would not be disturbed.

**Question:** Do you have a room or a corner of a room which is your place to pray? Do you purposefully get up early to pray so that you will not be distracted by the phone or by other people?

_____
_____
_____
_____
_____

## WEEK #33: Friday, _____

*"Moreover when ye fast, be not, as the hypocrites, of a sad countenance: for they disfigure their faces, that they may appear unto men to fast. Verily I say unto you, They have their reward. But thou, when thou fastest, anoint thine head, and wash thy face; That thou appear not unto men to fast, but unto thy Father which is in secret: and thy Father, which seeth in secret, shall reward thee openly."*
Matthew 6:16-18

**Thought:** God expects us to fast in order to discipline our human desires. However, we should not advertise the fact that we are fasting; we should do it unto God.

**Question:** When you are fasting, does everyone know, or do you keep it to yourself so that God can reward you?

_____

_____

_____

_____

## WEEK #33: Saturday, _____

*"And when they had ordained them elders in every church, and had prayed with fasting, they commended them to the Lord, on whom they believed."*
Acts 14:23

**Thought:** It is important to pray before making any big decisions. Fasting combined with prayer is even more effective, because we are more in tune with God.

**Question:** Do you fast and pray when you have a decision to make?

_____

_____

_____

_____

_____

*"He saw in a vision evidently about the ninth hour of the day an angel of God coming in to him, and saying unto him, Cornelius...And he said unto him, Thy prayers and thine alms are come up for a memorial before God."*
Acts 10:3-4

**Thought:** God keeps track of your prayers, and does not forget any of them. Praying is like making deposits in the bank of heaven!

**Question:** Have you been faithful in prayer? Do you realize that your prayers are building a memorial and when you need to draw on them, there will be something there to help you?

_____
_____
_____
_____

## WEEK #33: REVIEW

### This Week's Goal:
*Learn to discipline yourself to pray and fast.*

### This Week's Verse:
*"...If ye have faith as a grain of mustard seed, ye shall say unto this mountain, Remove hence to yonder place; and it shall remove; and nothing shall be impossible unto you. Howbeit this kind goeth not out but by prayer and fasting."*
Matthew 17:20-21

**Question:** Do you realize how important prayer and fasting is in your life? Have you made a commitment to do these things regularly?

_____
_____
_____
_____
_____

## STEP 9: Developing Self-Discipline
## Week 34 — Dates: _____

### This Week's Goal:
*Understand the importance of regular Bible study.*

### This Week's Verse:
*"As newborn babes, desire the sincere milk of
the word, that ye may grow thereby: If so be ye
have tasted that the Lord is gracious."*
1 Peter 2:2-3

If prayer is our spiritual water, then God's Word is our spiritual food. We need a regular intake of His Word in order to grow and be healthy spiritually. It is not enough to hear the Bible taught and preached by other people. God also expects us to study His Word for ourselves; to dig into it and discover the treasures it holds.

Extroverts who find it easy to pray may find it difficult to sit and study their Bible, but it is a spiritual discipline that must be developed in order to grow in the Lord. There are many resources available such as Bible reading charts, "one-year Bibles", and devotional books. Find something that works for you, and make Bible study a daily habit!

| Prayer Requests | Answers to Prayer | Thanksgiving and Praise |
|---|---|---|
|  |  |  |
|  |  |  |
|  |  |  |
|  |  |  |
|  |  |  |
|  |  |  |
|  |  |  |

## WEEK #34: Monday, _____

*"As newborn babes, desire the sincere milk of
the word, that ye may grow thereby: If so be ye
have tasted that the Lord is gracious."*
1 Peter 2:2-3

**Thought:** Just as a baby reaches for a bottle of milk because of
the remembered taste, so we should crave the Word of God.

**Question:** Have you developed a desire to study God's Word
because it has tasted so good to you spiritually?

_____
_____
_____
_____
_____
_____
_____

## WEEK #34: Tuesday, _____

*"This is the covenant that I will make with them after
those days, saith the Lord, I will put my laws into their
hearts, and in their minds will I write them;"*
Hebrews 10:16

**Thought:** A steady diet of the Word of God will imprint His
laws upon our hearts, not just upon our minds.

**Question:** Are you letting God write His laws on your heart,
by studying the Bible and allowing it to affect your life?

_____
_____
_____
_____
_____
_____
_____

## WEEK #34: Wednesday, _____

*"And Jesus answered him, saying, It is written, That man shall not live by bread alone, but by every word of God."*
Luke 4:4

**Thought:** We need food to survive physically, but we need the Word of God to survive spiritually.

**Question:** When you get up in the morning, what is your first priority: to eat or to study God's Word?

_____

_____

_____

_____

_____

_____

_____


## WEEK #34: Thursday, _____

*"Search the scriptures; for in them ye think ye have eternal life: and they are they which testify of me."*
John 5:39

**Thought:** We know that the Bible contains instructions for our salvation, but it is also where we personally encounter Jesus.

**Question:** Have you studied your Bible just to find out how to be saved, or do you study it to get to know Jesus Christ better?

_____

_____

_____

_____

_____

_____

## WEEK #34: Friday, _____

*"And that from a child thou hast known the holy
scriptures, which are able to make thee wise unto
salvation through faith which is in Christ Jesus."*
2 Timothy 3:15

**Thought:** Bible study should be a lifelong habit, and we should help our children establish it when they are young.

**Question:** How long have you been studying your Bible? Are you conscious of helping your children develop the habit of daily Bible study?

_____

_____

_____

_____

_____

_____

## WEEK #34: Saturday, _____

*"Study to shew thyself approved unto God,
a workman that needeth not to be ashamed,
rightly dividing the word of truth."*
2 Timothy 2:15

**Thought:** God is pleased when we study His Word, and it will keep us from doing things that will bring shame to Him.

**Question:** Do your Bible study habits bring God pleasure? Have they kept you from doing wrong things?

_____

_____

_____

_____

_____

_____

*"This book of the law shall not depart out of thy
mouth; but thou shalt meditate therein day and night,
that thou mayest observe to do according to all that is
written therein: for then thou shalt make thy way
prosperous, and then thou shalt have good success."*
Joshua 1:8

**Thought:** God has given us the recipe for success, and it is to meditate on His Word and obey it.

**Question:** Have you tried to build your own success, or have you built your life around God's Word and let Him prosper you?

_____

_____

_____

_____

## WEEK #34: REVIEW

### This Week's Goal:
*Understand the importance of regular Bible study.*

### This Week's Verse:
*"As newborn babes, desire the sincere milk of
the word, that ye may grow thereby: If so be ye
have tasted that the Lord is gracious."*
1 Peter 2:2-3

**Question:** What have you learned this week about the importance of regular Bible study? Did you realize how integral it was to your spiritual life? What is your plan to build personal Bible study into your daily schedule?

_____

_____

_____

_____

_____

# STEP 9: Developing Self-Discipline
## Week 35 — Dates: _____

### This Week's Goal:
*Discipline yourself to be a good
steward of what God has given you.*

### This Week's Verse:
*"Let a man so account of us, as of the ministers of
Christ, and stewards of the mysteries of God. Moreover
it is required in stewards, that a man be found faithful."*
1 Corinthians 4:1-2

God has given us many resources that He expects us to use wisely in our service to Him. A steward is a manager, not an owner. We need to remember that God has loaned us things to be used for His kingdom, not to be wasted or used selfishly. He is looking for faithfulness and will reward it with even more responsibility.

Some of the resources we are stewards over are: time, finances, talents, energy and relationships. We did not create these things on our own; they came from God. When we see these things as loans from God, we will be more likely to develop them and use them wisely.

| Prayer Requests | Answers to Prayer | Thanksgiving and Praise |
|---|---|---|
|  |  |  |
|  |  |  |
|  |  |  |
|  |  |  |
|  |  |  |
|  |  |  |
|  |  |  |

## WEEK #35: Monday, _____

*"Let a man so account of us, as of the ministers of
Christ, and stewards of the mysteries of God. Moreover
it is required in stewards, that a man be found faithful."*
1 Corinthians 4:1-2

**Thought:** We are stewards of what God has given us, and He expects us to be faithful in managing these things.

**Question:** What has God given you to manage? Have you been a faithful steward in these areas?

_____
_____
_____
_____
_____
_____
_____

## WEEK #35: Tuesday, _____

*"Walk in wisdom toward them that
are without, redeeming the time."*
Colossians 4:5

**Thought:** Each of us has 24 hours to use every day. God expects us to plan our time wisely and not to waste it.

**Question:** If you were to write down how you spend each of your 24 hours in a given day, how much of it is being used wisely in a way God would be pleased with?

_____
_____
_____
_____
_____
_____
_____

## WEEK #35: Wednesday, _____

*"He that is faithful in that which is least is faithful also in much: and he that is unjust in the least is unjust also in much. If therefore ye have not been faithful in the unrighteous mammon, who will commit to your trust the true riches?"*
Luke 16:10-11

**Thought:** It takes money to live, and it takes money to further the work of God. God expects us to be wise money managers.

**Question:** Have you faithfully managed the money God has given you? Do you follow His direction about how to use your finances, and are you careful not to waste them?

_____
_____
_____
_____
_____
_____

## WEEK #35: Thursday, _____

*"And they spake unto Moses, saying, The people bring much more than enough for the service of the work, which the LORD commanded to make."*
Exodus 36:5

**Thought:** God has given each of us abilities, which are to be used to further His kingdom and bring Him glory.

**Question:** Do you use your abilities for selfish gain, or do you use them to further the kingdom of God?

_____
_____
_____
_____
_____
_____

## WEEK #35: Friday, _____

*"And whatsoever ye do, do it heartily, as to the Lord, and not unto men; Knowing that of the Lord ye shall receive the reward of the inheritance: for ye serve the Lord Christ."*
Colossians 3:23-24

**Thought:** God has given us energy to use. We can do a task half-heartedly, or we can give it our best. He is pleased when we do our best!

**Question:** Do you use your energy to do your very best work for the kingdom of God?

_____
_____
_____
_____
_____
_____

## WEEK #35: Saturday, _____

*"And let us consider one another to provoke unto love and to good works:"*
Hebrews 10:24

**Thought:** Each of us have relationships with people who listen to what we say. We need to use our influence wisely.

**Question:** There are people in your life over whom you have influence. Do you use that influence to encourage them to do what is right?

_____
_____
_____
_____
_____
_____

*"His lord said unto him, Well done, good and faithful servant; thou hast been faithful over a few things, I will make thee ruler over many things: enter thou into the joy of thy lord."*
Matthew 25:23

**Thought:** If you are a faithful steward of what God has given you, He will trust you with more responsibilities.

**Question:** Have you been faithful in managing the resources God has given you? Have you been trusted with additional responsibilities?

_____
_____
_____
_____
_____

## WEEK #35: REVIEW

### This Week's Goal:
*Discipline yourself to be a good steward of what God has given you.*

### This Week's Verse:
*"Let a man so account of us, as of the ministers of Christ, and stewards of the mysteries of God. Moreover it is required in stewards, that a man be found faithful."*
1 Corinthians 4:1-2

**Question:** What have you learned about stewardship this week? Are there any areas in which you need to be a better steward? What changes will you make in these areas?

_____
_____
_____
_____
_____

## STEP 9: Developing Self-Discipline
### Week 36 — Dates: _____

**This Week's Goal:**
*Realize the importance of holiness in your lifestyle.*

**This Week's Verse:**
*"But as he which hath called you is holy, so be
ye holy in all manner of conversation; Because
it is written, Be ye holy; for I am holy."*
1 Peter 1:15-16

An important aspect of self-discipline is living a holy lifestyle. God is a holy God, and we are to reflect His holiness in the way we act, look, talk and think. Without a disciplined attitude in these areas, we will be easily swayed by popular thinking and advertising. Just about anything is "acceptable" in today's society, but that does not make it acceptable to God.

Holiness starts on the inside, with a pure heart and proper motives. True holiness is a result of being full of the Holy Spirit. Holiness will show on the outside and will be visible to those around us. God has called us to be separate and distinct from those of the world. A holy lifestyle is beautiful, clean and admirable.

| Prayer Requests | Answers to Prayer | Thanksgiving and Praise |
|---|---|---|
|  |  |  |
|  |  |  |
|  |  |  |
|  |  |  |
|  |  |  |
|  |  |  |
|  |  |  |

**WEEK #36: Monday, _____**

*"But as he which hath called you is holy,
so be ye holy in all manner of conversation;
Because it is written, Be ye holy; for I am holy."*
1 Peter 1:15-16

**Thought:** God is holy, and He has called us to be like Him. Holiness affects every facet of our lifestyle.

**Question:** Is God your example of holiness or do you measure yourself against someone else?

_____

_____

_____

_____

_____

_____

_____


**WEEK #36: Tuesday, _____**

*"Who shall ascend into the hill of the LORD?
or who shall stand in his holy place? He that hath
clean hands, and a pure heart; who hath not lifted
up his soul unto vanity, nor sworn deceitfully."*
Psalm 24:3-4

**Thought:** Holiness starts with a heart that is pure before God; a heart that has been cleansed of anything wrong.

**Question:** Is your heart clean before God? Do you search your heart daily and ask Him to show you any wrong attitudes?

_____

_____

_____

_____

_____

_____

## WEEK #36: Wednesday, _____

*"Finally, brethren, whatsoever things are true,*
*whatsoever things are honest, whatsoever things are just,*
*whatsoever things are pure, whatsoever things are lovely,*
*whatsoever things are of good report; if there be any virtue,*
*and if there be any praise, think on these things."*
Philippians 4:8

**Thought:** God expects our minds to be holy. When we are tempted with wrong thoughts, we need to refocus on something good.

**Question:** Are you conscious of not dwelling on wrong thoughts that come to your mind? Do you deliberately think about things that are pleasing to God?

_____
_____
_____
_____


## WEEK #36: Thursday, _____

*"But fornication, and all uncleanness, or covetousness, let it*
*not be once named among you, as becometh saints."*
Ephesians 5:3

**Thought:** True inner holiness is revealed in outward behaviour which is moral and honest, and which honours God. We need to guard our reputation for the sake of the Gospel.

**Question:** Are you known as a moral and honest person? Are you careful to avoid actions that would cause people to question your Christianity?

_____
_____
_____
_____
_____

*"Neither filthiness, nor foolish talking, nor jesting,
which are not convenient: but rather giving of thanks."*
Ephesians 5:4

**Thought:** True inner holiness is revealed in holy conversation. We need to avoid foolish, suggestive or questionable topics of conversation.

**Question:** Is your conversation holy? Do you discipline your mouth to keep from speaking unholy things?

_____

_____

_____

_____

_____

_____


WEEK #36: Saturday, _____

*"Flee also youthful lusts: but follow
righteousness, faith, charity, peace, with them that
call on the Lord out of a pure heart."*
2 Timothy 2:22

**Thought:** There are many things surrounding us every day that try to catch our attention and cause us to lust after what we should not have.

**Question:** Do you consciously turn your thoughts to God when you are tempted to lust after something?

_____

_____

_____

_____

_____

_____

## WEEK #36: Sunday, _____

*"But fornication, and all uncleanness, or covetousness,*
*let it not be once named among you, as becometh saints;"*
Ephesians 5:3

**Thought:** God commands us to keep ourselves morally and sexually pure.

**Question:** Have you set boundaries for yourself that keep you from falling into the trap of immorality?

_____

_____

_____

_____

_____

_____

_____


## WEEK #36: REVIEW

### This Week's Goal:
*Realize the importance of holiness in your lifestyle.*

### This Week's Verse:
*"But as he which hath called you is holy, so be*
*ye holy in all manner of conversation; Because*
*it is written, Be ye holy; for I am holy."*
1 Peter 1:15-16

**Question:** What have you learned this week about true holiness? Have you been made aware of any changes you need to make in your lifestyle?

_____

_____

_____

_____

_____

_____

# ORDER MY STEPS
## Devotional Journal

## STEP 10:
## Becoming
## Friends with God

# STEP 10: Becoming Friends with God

Now that you are developing self-discipline and good spiritual habits, you are probably settling into a daily routine that honours God and increases your effectiveness in His kingdom. However, your walk with God must never become just a dry routine! The way you prevent that from happening is to become friends with God. This does not imply a casual attitude or taking the Lord for granted. If that is your idea of friendship, perhaps you need to re-examine it. Deep and lasting friendships add so much to life, because they are based on solid foundations.

We will be looking at four attributes of real friendships and how these can be applied to our relationship with God. First of all, friends spend time together. Secondly, friends listen and communicate. A third attribute of friendship is trust. Finally, friends are loyal to each other.

| Area of your life to evaluate: | Weak, Good or Great |
|---|---|
| Relationship with God as your Father | |
| Emotional and physical condition | |
| Self-image and purpose in life | |
| Development of gifts and abilities | |
| Awareness of others' needs | |
| Reaching out to others | |
| Recognizing God's voice | |
| Obeying God's direction | |
| Self-discipline and spiritual habits | |
| Relationship with God as your friend | |

God wants to be your friend! This is a lifetime friendship that will bring you constant joy.

## STEP 10: Becoming Friends with God
### Week 37 — Dates: _____

### This Week's Goal:
*Understand the importance of spending time with God.*

### This Week's Verse:
*"Ye are my friends, if ye do whatsoever I command you. Henceforth I call you not servants; for the servant knoweth not what his lord doeth: but I have called you friends; for all things that I have heard of my Father I have made known unto you."*
John 15:14-15

An important aspect of friendship is spending time together. Friends take time, make time, find time...because they enjoy each other's company. Our friendship with God involves spending a lot of time together. As we get to know Him better, we will enjoy His company more and more, and will make spending time with Him a priority in our lives.

Jesus wants to spend time with you! He knocks politely on the door of your heart and calls to you. Then He waits for you to hear Him and come open the door. Once you extend the invitation to come in, He does so, and you can have sweet fellowship with Him. We need to learn to keep our heart's door open for Jesus at all times.

| Prayer Requests | Answers to Prayer | Thanksgiving and Praise |
|---|---|---|
|  |  |  |
|  |  |  |
|  |  |  |
|  |  |  |
|  |  |  |
|  |  |  |
|  |  |  |

## WEEK #37: Monday, _____

*"Ye are my friends, if ye do whatsoever I command you. Henceforth I call you not servants; for the servant knoweth not what his lord doeth: but I have called you friends; for all things that I have heard of my Father I have made known unto you."*
John 15:14-15

**Thought:** We start our Christian walk as servants, but as we get to know God better and become more aware of His work on the earth, we move into a friendship with Him.

**Question:** Are you aware of what God is trying to accomplish on the earth? Do you feel like you are becoming friends with God?

_____

_____

_____

_____

_____


## WEEK #37: Tuesday, _____

*"For there is no difference between the Jew and the Greek: for the same Lord over all is rich unto all that call upon him."*
Romans 10:12

**Thought:** In the Old Testament, God dealt mainly with the Jews, but since the day of Pentecost, anyone can have a relationship with Him.

**Question:** Do you appreciate the privilege of having a close personal relationship with God?

_____

_____

_____

_____

_____

_____

## WEEK #37: Wednesday, _____

*"Behold, I stand at the door, and knock: if any man hear my voice, and open the door, I will come in to him, and will sup with him, and he with me."*
Revelation 3:20

**Thought:** God wants to spend time with you, but He waits for your invitation.

**Question:** Do you listen closely for God's knock on your heart's door? Do you let Him in and spend time with Him?

_____
_____
_____
_____
_____

## WEEK #37: Thursday, _____

*"If we say that we have fellowship with him, and walk in darkness, we lie, and do not the truth: But if we walk in the light, as he is in the light, we have fellowship one with another, and the blood of Jesus Christ his Son cleanseth us from all sin."*
1 John 1:6-7

**Thought:** We must be walking in God's direction in order to have fellowship with Him. We cannot spend time together and continue to do things that offend Him.

**Question:** Have you made a conscious effort to rid your life of anything offensive to God, so that you can spend time with Him?

_____
_____
_____
_____
_____

## WEEK #37: Friday, _____

*"And the Spirit and the bride say, Come. And let him that heareth say, Come. And let him that is athirst come. And whosoever will, let him take the water of life freely."*
Revelation 22:17

**Thought:** God puts no limit on the time you can spend with Him. It is a free gift that is yours for the taking.

**Question:** Do you take advantage of the privilege of spending time with your best Friend? Do you daily answer His invitation to come into His presence?

_____

_____

_____

_____

_____

## WEEK #37: Saturday, _____

*"Because he hath set his love upon me, therefore will I deliver him: I will set him on high, because he hath known my name. He shall call upon me, and I will answer him: I will be with him in trouble; I will deliver him, and honour him. With long life will I satisfy him, and shew him my salvation."*
Psalm 91:14-16

**Thought:** God reserves special treatment for those who will set their love upon Him. When you choose Him as a friend, it will reap abundant blessings in your life.

**Question:** Have you set your love upon God? Have you chosen to make Him the object of your affections?

_____

_____

_____

_____

_____

*"That I may know him, and the power of his resurrection, and the fellowship of his sufferings, being made conformable unto his death;"*
Philippians 3:10

**Thought:** Getting to know God involves identifying with His suffering, not just looking for blessings.

**Question:** Have you decided that you want to get to know God better, regardless of the cost?

_____

_____

_____

_____

_____

## WEEK #37: REVIEW

### This Week's Goal:
*Understand the importance of spending time with God.*

### This Week's Verse:
*"Ye are my friends, if ye do whatsoever I command you. Henceforth I call you not servants; for the servant knoweth not what his lord doeth: but I have called you friends; for all things that I have heard of my Father I have made known unto you."*
John 15:14-15

**Question:** Has your study this week shown you the importance of spending time with God, to get to know Him better? Have you made it a priority in your schedule?

_____

_____

_____

_____

_____

## STEP 10: Becoming Friends with God
Week 38 — Dates: _____

### This Week's Goal:
*Develop your communication with God.*

### This Week's Verse:
*"I love the LORD, because he hath heard my voice and
my supplications. Because he hath inclined his ear unto
me, therefore will I call upon him as long as I live."*
Psalm 116:1-2

True friends communicate with each other. Regardless of
busy schedules or distance between them, they will find a
way to talk and to listen to each other. Our friendship with
God depends on both the quantity and the quality of our
communication.

We need to be attentive listeners when God is speaking to
us. He has promised that He will speak! There is so much we
can learn from our conversations with God. We also need to
talk to God regularly, about every situation in our lives. He
should be the first one we go to when we are concerned about
something. He also should be the first one we want to share
our joy with over something wonderful that has happened in
our lives.

| Prayer Requests | Answers to Prayer | Thanksgiving and Praise |
|---|---|---|
|  |  |  |
|  |  |  |
|  |  |  |
|  |  |  |
|  |  |  |
|  |  |  |
|  |  |  |

## WEEK #38: Monday, _____

*"I love the LORD, because he hath heard my voice and my supplications. Because he hath inclined his ear unto me, therefore will I call upon him as long as I live."*
Psalm 116:1-2

**Thought:** We tend to talk to people who really listen to us. God is the best listener we can find!

**Question:** Do you get frustrated when people do not listen to you? Do you know you can talk to God about everything?

_____

_____

_____

_____

_____

_____

## WEEK #38: Tuesday, _____

*"Hear my cry, O God; attend unto my prayer. From the end of the earth will I cry unto thee, when my heart is overwhelmed: lead me to the rock that is higher than I. For thou hast been a shelter for me, and a strong tower from the enemy."*
Psalm 61:1-3

**Thought:** God will be there for us when we are going through a tough time. He is always ready to listen.

**Question:** Who do you go to first when you are upset? Do you take your problems and concerns to God?

_____

_____

_____

_____

_____

_____

## WEEK #38: Wednesday, _____

*"I cried unto God with my voice, even unto*
*God with my voice; and he gave ear unto me."*
Psalm 77:1

**Thought:** David was not afraid to express his deepest emotions to God. He knew He would listen.

**Question:** Are you honest in your communication with God? Do you tell Him exactly how you feel, remembering that you cannot hide anything from Him anyway?

_____
_____
_____
_____
_____
_____

## WEEK #38: Thursday, _____

*"As for me, I will call upon God; and the LORD shall*
*save me. Evening, and morning, and at noon, will I*
*pray, and cry aloud: and he shall hear my voice."*
Psalm 55:16-17

**Thought:** When we are with friends, we talk throughout the day. We do not set a beginning and ending time for our conversations.

**Question:** Have you limited your conversations with God to a time slot each day, or are you conscious of communicating with Him as you go about your daily activities as well?

_____
_____
_____
_____
_____

**WEEK #38: Friday, _____**

*"Then shall ye call upon me, and ye shall go and pray unto
me, and I will hearken unto you. And ye shall seek me, and
find me, when ye shall search for me with all your heart."*
Jeremiah 29:12-13

**Thought:** Some people think God is hard to find, but it
could be that they have not yet put their whole heart into a
relationship with Him.

**Question:** Do you seek God's presence with your whole
heart? Is it a high priority to you to talk to Him regularly?

_____
_____
_____
_____
_____
_____

**WEEK #38: Saturday, _____**

*"The LORD is nigh unto all them that call upon him, to all
that call upon him in truth. He will fulfil the desire of them
that fear him: he also will hear their cry, and will save them."*
Psalm 145:18-19

**Thought:** God promises to hear us when we call on Him in
truth. He expects honesty and respect from us.

**Question:** When you talk to God, is your honesty balanced
with respect for who He is?

_____
_____
_____
_____
_____
_____

_"My sheep hear my voice, and I know them, and they follow me: And I give unto them eternal life; and they shall never perish, neither shall any man pluck them out of my hand."_
John 10:27-28

**Thought:** Just as sheep learn to recognize the voice of their particular shepherd over time, we become familiar with the voice of God as we get to know Him better.

**Question:** Do you feel like you recognize God's voice because you have spent time communicating with Him?

_____
_____
_____
_____
_____

## WEEK #38: REVIEW

### This Week's Goal:
_Develop your communication with God._

### This Week's Verse:
_"I love the LORD, because he hath heard my voice and my supplications. Because he hath inclined his ear unto me, therefore will I call upon him as long as I live."_
Psalm 116:1-2

**Question:** Through this week's study, have you seen any areas you need to work on in your communication with God? What are you going to do differently?

_____
_____
_____
_____
_____
_____

## STEP 10: Becoming Friends with God
## Week 39 — Dates: _____

### This Week's Goal:
*Realize the importance of trust in your relationship with God.*

### This Week's Verse:
*"And the scripture was fulfilled which saith, Abraham
believed God, and it was imputed unto him for
righteousness: and he was called the Friend of God."*
James 2:23

Friends trust each other! Abraham trusted God through the many trials and tests of his life, and God trusted him enough to call him His friend. Trust is foundational to a friendship, but lasting trust does not happen overnight. We build trust by going through life experiences together — both happy and sad.

When we first become Christians, we take a step of faith. Faith in God is believing in His power to save us and to act on our behalf. Trust, however, implies a confidence in God to do what is best for us, whether we understand it or not. Trusting God is believing that He has our best interests at heart, and that anything He allows in our lives is for our good. We need to learn to trust God, and to be faithful so that He can trust us.

| Prayer Requests | Answers to Prayer | Thanksgiving and Praise |
|---|---|---|
| | | |
| | | |
| | | |
| | | |
| | | |
| | | |
| | | |

## WEEK #39: Monday, _____

*"And the scripture was fulfilled which saith,*
*Abraham believed God, and it was imputed unto him for*
*righteousness: and he was called the Friend of God."*
James 2:23

**Thought:** It was Abraham's strong trust in God that caused God to call him His friend.

**Question:** Do you have a deep and settled trust in God? Would God be able to call you His friend?

_____
_____
_____
_____
_____
_____

## WEEK #39: Tuesday, _____

*"It is better to trust in the LORD than to put*
*confidence in man. It is better to trust in the*
*LORD than to put confidence in princes."*
Psalm 118:8-9

**Thought:** If we put all of our trust and confidence in human beings, we will be disappointed at some point. We need to place our trust in the Lord.

**Question:** Have you ever been disappointed by someone you trusted? Did it cause you to lean more heavily on God?

_____
_____
_____
_____
_____
_____

## WEEK #39: Wednesday, _____

*"But let all those that put their trust in thee rejoice:*
*let them ever shout for joy, because thou defendest them:*
*let them also that love thy name be joyful in thee."*
Psalm 5:11

**Thought:** It is a tremendous privilege to be able to trust in God. When we do, we have access to incredible protection.

**Question:** Do you realize what a privilege it is to trust in God? Have you experienced His protection?

_____
_____
_____
_____
_____
_____

## WEEK #39: Thursday, _____

*"Delight thyself also in the LORD; and he shall give*
*thee the desires of thine heart. Commit thy way unto the*
*LORD; trust also in him; and he shall bring it to pass."*
Psalm 37:4-5

**Thought:** Trust is not a chore; it is a joy. God wants us to trust Him completely so that He can bless us.

**Question:** Do you enjoy trusting God? Have you committed your life and plans completely to Him and are you letting Him guide your future?

_____
_____
_____
_____
_____
_____
_____

## WEEK #39: Friday, _____

*"And they that know thy name will put their trust in thee:
for thou, LORD, hast not forsaken them that seek thee."*
Psalm 9:10

**Thought:** When we place our trust in God, we can be assured
that He will never forsake us.

**Question:** Do you realize that when you made a lifetime
commitment to God, He made a lifetime commitment to
you?

_____

_____

_____

_____

_____


## WEEK #39: Saturday, _____

*"Now the God of peace...Make you perfect in every
good work to do his will, working in you that which
is wellpleasing in his sight, through Jesus Christ;
to whom be glory for ever and ever. Amen."*
Hebrews 13:20-21

**Thought:** God will not abandon you halfway through your
journey with Him. You can trust Him to be with you through
the whole process of becoming more like Him.

**Question:** Do you trust God to stay with you through your
entire life's journey? Do you realize He has started a work in
you and intends to finish it?

_____

_____

_____

_____

_____

*"And the LORD said unto Satan, Hast thou considered my servant Job, that there is none like him in the earth, a perfect and an upright man, one that feareth God, and escheweth evil? and still he holdeth fast his integrity, although thou movedst me against him, to destroy him without cause."*
Job 2:3

**Thought:** Job had made a lifetime commitment to God that did not waver even when multiple tragedies struck his life. God was able to trust Job to be faithful to Him.

**Question:** Can God trust you to be faithful to Him through your whole life, including the good and the bad times?

_____

_____

_____

_____

## WEEK #39: REVIEW

### This Week's Goal:
*Realize the importance of trust in your relationship with God.*

### This Week's Verse:
*"And the scripture was fulfilled which saith, Abraham believed God, and it was imputed unto him for righteousness: and he was called the Friend of God."*
James 2:23

**Question:** What did you learn about trust this week? Do you feel that you have a relationship of trust, both ways, between you and God?

_____

_____

_____

_____

_____

## STEP 10: Becoming Friends with God
**Week 40 — Dates:** _____

### This Week's Goal:
*Discover the importance of loyalty
in your relationship with God.*

### This Week's Verse:
*"And thou shalt love the Lord thy God with all thy heart,
and with all thy soul, and with all thy mind, and with
all thy strength: this is the first commandment."*
Mark 12:30

True friends are loyal to each other. They will not forsake each other no matter what happens or what others might say or do. It should be the same in our relationship with God. When we become Christians, we make a commitment until death. We become completely God's, belonging to no one else.

If we try to give God half of our heart, we will lose focus and become confused. True joy is found only when we give Him 100% of everything we have. God is pleased with those who are loyal to Him. He has promised to be loyal to us as well, and we can bank on that promise! He will always be there for us.

| Prayer Requests | Answers to Prayer | Thanksgiving and Praise |
|---|---|---|
| | | |
| | | |
| | | |
| | | |
| | | |
| | | |
| | | |

*"And thou shalt love the Lord thy God with all thy heart, and with all thy soul, and with all thy mind, and with all thy strength: this is the first commandment."*
Mark 12:30

**Thought:** God expects us to love Him with everything we have, holding nothing back.

**Question:** Do you love God completely, with your entire heart, soul, mind and strength?

_____

_____

_____

_____

_____

_____

_____

*"No servant can serve two masters: for either he will hate the one, and love the other; or else he will hold to the one, and despise the other. Ye cannot serve God and mammon."*
Luke 16:13

**Thought:** We cannot serve God with part of our heart and follow other pursuits with the rest of our heart.

**Question:** Are you focused completely on serving God, or are your loyalties stretched in several directions?

_____

_____

_____

_____

_____

_____

_____

*"A man that hath friends must shew himself friendly: and there is a friend that sticketh closer than a brother."*
Proverbs 18:24

**Thought:** As close as we are to our family members, God is even closer to us.

**Question:** Are you close to your siblings? Do you realize that God can be even closer to you than that?

_____
_____
_____
_____
_____
_____
_____

*"For a day in thy courts is better than a thousand. I had rather be a doorkeeper in the house of my God, than to dwell in the tents of wickedness."*
Psalm 84:10

**Thought:** Even our worst days with God are better than our best days were without Him.

**Question:** Are you loyal to God even when things are not going as well as you would like?

_____
_____
_____
_____
_____
_____
_____

## WEEK #40: Friday, _____

*"Cast not away therefore your confidence,*
*which hath great recompence of reward. For ye*
*have need of patience, that, after ye have done the*
*will of God, ye might receive the promise."*
Hebrews 10:35-36

**Thought:** If we will be faithful to God even through rough times, at the end we will receive a wonderful reward.

**Question:** Have you stayed loyal to God through the trials and temptations of your life? Are you looking forward to the heavenly reward that is waiting for you?

_____
_____
_____
_____
_____


## WEEK #40: Saturday, _____

*"...for he hath said, I will never leave thee, nor forsake*
*thee. So that we may boldly say, The Lord is my helper,*
*and I will not fear what man shall do unto me."*
Hebrews 13:5-6

**Thought:** God will be loyal to His children forever. He has promised to stay beside us, so we do not need to fear anything that happens in our lives.

**Question:** Do you realize that God will never leave you nor forsake you? Do you find comfort in that?

_____
_____
_____
_____
_____

## WEEK #40: Sunday, _____

*"For I know the thoughts that I think toward
you, saith the LORD, thoughts of peace, and
not of evil, to give you an expected end."*
Jeremiah 29:11

**Thought:** God has a beautiful future full of peace planned for us. We can count on His loyalty!

**Question:** Are you convinced of God's loyalty to you? Are you aware of the future He has planned for you — eternal life and joy forever?

_____
_____
_____
_____
_____

## WEEK #40: REVIEW

### This Week's Goal:
*Discover the importance of loyalty
in your relationship with God.*

### This Week's Verse:
*"And thou shalt love the Lord thy God with all thy heart,
and with all thy soul, and with all thy mind, and with
all thy strength: this is the first commandment."*
Mark 12:30

**Question:** What have you learned this week about loyalty in your relationship with God? Have you promised to be faithful to God until death?

_____
_____
_____
_____
_____

# ORDER MY STEPS
# Conclusion

Have you enjoyed this devotional journal? Growth is sometimes painful, sometimes exciting, but always necessary. Anything that is not growing is dying.

You have learned many things that will help you in your spiritual journey. There are many more things to learn. I hope that you now have more tools to dig into the Bible and prayer to discover things for yourself.

We can never exhaust the wisdom of God. Until the day we are taken up to heaven, there will always be something new He wants to teach us. He is deeper than the deepest ocean and higher than the highest mountain. Let's keep growing together!

| Area of your life to evaluate: | Weak, Good or Great |
|---|---|
| Relationship with God as your Father | |
| Emotional and physical condition | |
| Self-image and purpose in life | |
| Development of gifts and abilities | |
| Awareness of others' needs | |
| Reaching out to others | |
| Recognizing God's voice | |
| Obeying God's direction | |
| Self-discipline and spiritual habits | |
| Relationship with God as your friend | |

# MY GOALS FOR THE COMING YEAR:

(If you write them down, it will keep you accountable.)

1. _____
_____

2. _____
_____

3. _____
_____

4. _____
_____

5. _____
_____

6. _____
_____

7. _____
_____

8. _____
_____

9. _____
_____

10. _____
_____

Made in the USA
Lexington, KY
29 November 2018